Testimonials

In this beautifully written book, Joan Portman brings the authentic meaning of healing environments to the reader just as she did to a major medical center in the Philadelphia region. With poignant and tender stories, Joan narrates the importance of treating occupants in a hospital bed (who surely do not want to be there) with as much empathy and consideration as they deserve—even the ones who are difficult and bad-tempered. This is a good read for anyone, but especially for someone with a loved one who may be getting treatment for a life-altering illness. And I would recommend it to doctors, nurses, medical students, and hospital administrators. It is an important topic and crucial for those who need to understand the complexities of what a person who is ill is experiencing. Even the simplest—like a special blanket, a pillow, or a teddy bear—as well as major hospital environment improvements—such as healing gardens and quiet, comfortable spaces where patients and their family members can sit and think—can be restorative for their patients. Joan shows us, too, that learning how to truly listen is one of the greatest gifts to give a patient. Joan did her beloved father-in-love proud with this excellent book that speaks to all our hearts.

Marie Murphy Duess
Marketing and Communications Specialist and
author of numerous history books and novels.

A brilliantly written series of real-life stories of how ordinary people can make an extraordinary difference under the most difficult circumstances.

You'll feel like you are standing in the room as you read these emotional vignettes. It makes you grateful for all you have, teaches, and inspires you how you too can make a difference.

Steven Weinick,
Senior Vice President
PepsiCo Global
Research and Development/Retired

This book is an amazing tribute to the healing power of connection. The connections we make human-to-human. In *Creative Healing Places*, Joan Portman has been blessed to share intimate healing stories that touch the soul. Her prose allows us to feel, hear, and see the experiences documented in this book. Not only is it a read you cannot put down, but it will be a resource to revisit for its wisdom, its truth, and its splendor.

Yvette E. Taylor, Esquire
Probate and Estate Administration Lawyer

Everything about this book is right and righteous. It affirms the harmony of faith communities working together while affirming that every human soul is worthy of being treated in a godly manner. Through the many scenarios encountered, the reader will come to extract a deeper essence of hospitals, not only as a place of medical care, but also as one being gracious of spirit.

Suffering, healing, and comfort, addressed in this collection, might be understood in an example by Thornton Wilder's novel, The Eighth Day. Wilder's words compare life's struggles to a tapestry. Looked at from the underside, one will find short and long colored threads, erratically placed with no sense of order or design. The view from the top side is much more pleasing to the eye, where all threads are intricately placed. Wilder's 'thesis' is that God purposely places threads for a greater purpose. While, at times, our lives seem to be represented by the underside, God's vantage point above it is a masterpiece. Our role as comforters, God's partners in this world, is also part of the plan.

Through the supple story-telling hands of Joan Portman, we are guided gently through some of life's most delicate moments. The work and dedication of the volunteers who made this project come to fruition is impressive; the stories themselves are easily absorbed into our pathos. In reading this tender book, and taking it to heart, one will be inspired to live a life of "loving our neighbors as ourselves".

Cantor Steven Stoehr
President, Cantors Assembly Foundation

"Your grief is
the purest
love letter
that you can
ever send
to the one
you have lost
to death". John Roedel "Upon Departure"

Unless it is this treasure of a book written by the faithful daughter-in-law, Joan Portman, who honored the life and memory of her precious Father-in-Love during his 9-month journey with inoperable brain cancer.

Joan used her grief experience, her creative energy, her design skills, and her innate respect for the whole person to create The Healing Environments Program. Joan's story documents her mission to make life better for those who are ill or in their final days. As Cicely Saunders, founder of the hospice movement in London, says "You matter because you are you, and you matter to the end of your life. We will do all we can not only to help you die peacefully, but also to live until you die."

As a hospice medical director, I have witnessed what beautiful rooms, gardens, waterfalls, nondenominational chapel space, and music can do to ease patients and their family's anxiety and fear. I was privileged to visit patients in their homes. From each of those experiences I would take a fictional piece of cloth from which I will make my own quilt for when my time comes to make the journey which we all face.

Joan Portman's book is a poignant read about the quilt she is making.

Linda L. Coffin, MD
Former Hospice Medical Director
Home and Hospice Care of Rhode Island
(Now Hope Health)

Having been profoundly challenged by "life" for over thirty years with a son, physically vulnerable and fragile, I only wish "back then", I had the companionship of "Creative Healing Places". There is so much wisdom here; thoughtful insights, pragmatic suggestions, gentle storytelling, and a real-life lesson in transforming the culture and personality of healing institutions into communities of possibility and defiant hope.

Rabbi Charles S. Sherman,
Melrose B'nai Israel Emanu-El
author, *The Broken and The Whole*
Discovering Joy after Heartbreak
Lessons from a Life of Faith

I met Joan Portman several years ago when our group contributed blankets for her Healing Environments Program. I loved what the program encompassed regarding volunteers impacting the lives of patients in dire health situations.

Then came the book ... the true stories captured my heart! I love the 'blanket' theme - both literally and figuratively with each thread weaving care and kindness. The stories brought tears and moments of joy to my heart. This book should be read by all of us; it is one that will encourage us to take care of our loved ones in their time of need. Thank you, Joan for sharing your own experience with your Father-in-Love, where your story began, and where you created a wave of caring for others to do the same.

Carol Fenton, Founder and Leader,
Connect-the-DOTS charity

Creative Healing Places

STORIES OF HOPE, COMFORT, AND INSPIRATION

JOAN PORTMAN

CREATIVE HEALING PLACES:
Stories of Hope, Comfort, and Inspiration
by Joan Portman
1. BIO026000 **BIOGRAPHY & AUTOBIOGRAPHY** / Personal Memoirs
2. CRA022000 **CRAFTS & HOBBIES** / Needlework / General
3. HEA039030 **HEALTH & FITNESS** / Diseases & Conditions / Cancer
ISBN: 979-8-88636-010-3 (paperback)
ISBN: 979-8-88636-011-0 (ebook)

Library of Congress Control Number: 2022913486

Cover design by LEWIS AGRELL
Cover photographs by FRANK PRONESTI, Heirloom Studio

Printed in the United States of America

Authority Publishing
11230 Gold Express Dr. #310-413
Gold River, CA 95670
800-877-1097
www.AuthorityPublishing.com

Dedication

To My Wonderful and Amazing Husband, Ron,
My Rock, the Love of My Life, and My Best Friend!

To the entire Portman, Welch, Hall, Silver, Fried,
Hornstein, and Chacon Families.

To those who have come before, who inspired
and led me to this place, to those here now,
your love and support are my strength,
and to those yet to be born…

I pray that I live my life in such a way that you will
be inspired to pursue and achieve your dreams,
and to live your lives devoted to
goodness and kindness.

And to all the caregivers out there!

Table Of Contents

Foreword

When it's better for everyone, it's better for everyone.

– Eleanor Roosevelt, American political figure, diplomat
and activist, First Lady of the United States, 1933-1945

Foreword by Lillian Schonewolf, Vice President,
Community Health and Well-Being, Trinity,
Mid-Atlantic Region. Former Director of Volunteer
Services, St. Mary Medical Center.

Imagine you are a patient, and your illness has brought
you to the hospital. You are at the door to what will be
your room for the length of your stay. The floor and
ceiling are beige. The walls might be ivory or a light
pastel shade. The bed is neatly made, but the sheets
and blanket are white. Do you get a feeling of welcoming comfort or cold sterility?

Now imagine you are warmly tucked into bed with
a colorful patterned handmade afghan covering you,
a neck roll pillow gently supporting your head and

neck, and a bedside pocket pouch, all provided by a caring volunteer. (Pocket pouches are made to hold your phone, tablet, nurses' call button/TV remote, glasses, and other small items within easy reach.) These are only a few differences the *Healing Environments Program* made at St Mary Medical Center in Bucks County, Pennsylvania.

By introducing this program at St Mary, we were able to create a new atmosphere within our hospital rooms that changed the look *and* feel of the rooms. Control for selecting any enhancements was in the patients' hands, as we carefully listened to 'The Patient Voice.' Volunteers invited them to choose the color(s) and pattern of an afghan, fleece blanket, or quilt to warm them, soft hair-loss caps, and many other gifts. All were made by local crafters from vibrant yarns and fabrics. Community League of St Mary generously funded the program. As the program grew, patients and staff made suggestions for additional items, and many more handmade gifts were added to the selections. The person-to-person connection created by our crafters helped the patients realize people in our community were thinking of them and taking action to ease their suffering.

What effect did these acts of altruism have on the patients? As evidenced from their comments on our questionnaires (Appendix II) and those made to our volunteers and staff, we learned that they felt valued, less stressed, and comforted; their humanity was being honored as they received the tender care provided by the volunteers' visits and gifts. Many expressed amazement that people who didn't even know them devoted their time and shared their talents to create these special items!

The rooms were transformed. They became more personalized, places of serenity and healing, less clinical, and more the patients' private sanctuary where they could get cozy under *their* blanket and feel safe. The volunteers also offered a hand to hold, a listening ear, a reassuring presence, and a shoulder to cry on when needed.

The program also benefitted our medical staff. Many people go into medicine with a sincere desire to make a difference for patients. However, it is easy to become discouraged as the amount of work required during their shift does not permit medical professionals to give the quality time they would like to spend with patients. The significant aspects of the Healing Environments Program were human touch, conversations, and newly formed friendships, as the volunteers visited the patients.

Of course, the clinical teams are everyday heroes, the courageous frontliners. Still, so often, they have a tremendous amount to do to assure each of their patients receives what is needed. The COVID pandemic only served to put even more and greater demands on the medical staff and underscored the benefits and value of the Healing Environments concept. In the pre-pandemic era, there would be more laughter and joking heard in the units and the corridors. Friendly volunteers visited daily, bringing the healing cart filled to capacity with gifts. Patients came to look forward to these visits, a welcome break from the stress of a hospital stay. In addition to receiving the very best medical care, the volunteers uplifted patients' spirits. Unfortunately, COVID necessitated a halt to volunteer programs within the hospital. Patients and staff sorely missed these programs and participants alike.

The Healing Environments Program changed the hospital in significant ways. It made a dramatic difference for St Mary as a healthcare center within our community. It enabled us to become a true 'City of Healing' in all aspects, medical of course, but also environmental and emotional as we offered support to those experiencing health challenges, suffering, and loss.

This program also helped us remember why we chose to work in healthcare. We were reminded of our desire and intention to provide the very best in patient care through our excellent staff and the latest innovations in medical equipment and treatments. Moreover, we could enhance our patients' overall experience by treating the body, mind, and spirit as we accompanied them on their journey. Our devoted volunteers have continually shared their talents, abilities, and dedication to spreading goodwill throughout our community. What a difference!

The Healing Environments Program served our patients at critical times in their lives. Unique and purposeful opportunities for volunteers were made available. Our medical personnel received much-needed stress relief, and our hospital enjoyed years of award-winning recognition. When it was better for everyone, it was better for everyone.

Joan, as I sat with you and Helen that first day in my office while you explained your concept, my immediate thought was, *we have to do this!* And we did.

Author's Note

This book is a compilation of true stories about a group of volunteers, ordinary people, who made an extraordinary difference at St. Mary Medical Center. Over three hundred crafters worked off-site contributing 293,324 hours, creating 11,752 afghans, quilts, and blankets, and almost 27,000 other comfort items during the nine years of the program. More than fifty on-site volunteers visited the units throughout the hospital, offering these handmade gifts to 27,000 patients.

This human-to-human connection sent the clear message that they were cared about and not forgotten. Now we're sharing our insights and inspiration with you. It is my sincere desire that the messages related will provide ideas you can implement to enrich your own life or to help a loved one struck with serious illness or in need of some extra loving care.

Thank you for inviting us into your experience.

1

Harry, My Father-In-Love

How wonderful it is that nobody need wait a single moment before starting to improve the world.

– Anne Frank, German-born,
Dutch-Jewish diarist and Holocaust victim

Dedicated to Harry and Sylvia Portman (Sabah and Savtah)

Though this book is a collection of stories, it begins with one story, that of my Father-in Love who was truly like a father to me. He's also the reason the Healing Environments Program exists.

"Your father has brain tumors. I'm very sorry to say they're malignant." These words, spoken to my husband by the oncologist at Portsmouth Hospital in August of 2000, sent our lives into turmoil and began what was to become my father-in-law's nine-month battle with cancer.

Harry Portman was known fondly by many names and terms of endearment. His mother called him her "Diamond" and indeed he was a gem. He came naturally by his nickname "Red" due to his wavy red hair. From the time his first grandchild was born, we addressed him with love and respect as Sabah (Hebrew meaning grandfather). To me, he was my "Father-in-Love."

Harry was a *Tzadik* (a righteous person) and a humble man who believed in taking his best out into the world each day, sharing it with everyone he met. Some might say he led a normal, even common life. But the legacy of love and devotion he passed on to his family contradicts that notion.

Following World War II, he became the owner of Islington Street Market in Portsmouth, NH. It was a "mom-and-pop" corner grocery that carried everything from milk, bread, beer, and eggs to diapers, toys, and hardware. An item might be hanging in the rafters, but he had it and knew exactly where it was. The customers came, not so much because of his stock, but because of *him*. To know him was to love him. He had a great laugh, a handsome, open countenance that welcomed people to confide in him, sparkling blue eyes, and that beautiful hair. He was always ready with a joke, a kind word, queries about his customers' families; it was no wonder they would drive across town to visit the store (or "stoah" as he and his New England clientele pronounced it). As a die-hard Red Sox fan, he would commiserate with his customers over the team's recent loss or cheer its victories.

Sabah's Collage

From top left clockwise: Ringbearer, Young "Handsome Harry",
Army Warrant Officer (Links Trainer for pilots),
Shayna's First Dance

**To enjoy the photos throughout the book in color,
I invite you to the "Photo Gallery" section on my website,
Joan@joanportman.com**

On that hot August day, my husband Ron received the call informing him that Sabah had collapsed at our summer cottage in southern Maine and had been rushed to Portsmouth Hospital. An MRI revealed that undetected melanoma had caused tumors in his brain, paralyzing his right side. Ron flew from our home in Houston to Portsmouth and brought Sabah back to MD Anderson Cancer Center in Houston, where he was a patient for five weeks, followed by six weeks at TIRR, the physical therapy facility in the Houston Medical Center, relearning to walk and use his right side.

During the next months, as our devoted daughter, Shayna, or I drove him to his out-patient appointments, we would listen to his favorite CDs and sing along. One featured Louis Armstrong singing in his raspy baritone. Sabah's voice had been affected by the radiation treatments and he sounded as scratchy as old "Satchmo." He truly enjoyed his physical and occupational therapy sessions and loved to be active. He also enjoyed joking with the male therapists and flirting with his attractive young trainers, making them laugh. We found what enjoyment we could, as we waited hopefully for positive results.

Sabah's appetite was also affected during his treatments, and he lost a lot of weight. But he continued bravely without a complaint, without asking, "Why me?" The tumor shrank, but unfortunately more developed in other areas of the brain that could not be radiated without seriously impacting his quality of life. I can vividly remember his neurosurgeon, Dr. H, showing us the images of the tumors on his computer screen. He carefully and thoroughly explained the results and possible options. I was so grateful for his physician's empathy. My Father-in-Love wasn't just another brain cancer patient to him, but a human being going through an extremely stressful situation, who deserved and received kindness and understanding. The doctor left us to discuss options privately and to allow Sabah to decide what he wanted to do regarding his future. His decision was to cease further radiation in favor of quality of life over longevity. As sad as we were to come to this point, we knew it was the right choice.

The silver lining from this sad chapter in our lives was the birth of the Healing Environments Program concept. Ideas emerged from my deep desire to honor my Father-in-Love's battle with brain cancer and the enhancements I had made to his hospital room.

By presenting the Healing Environments concept to several Houston hospital CEOs, I was hopeful many other patients could benefit from similar changes to typical hospital rooms.

In addition to the modifications I made in Sabah's room, my proposal to these administrators included total renovation of the rooms and adjoining bathrooms.

The plans called for the introduction of muted, restful colors and mid-tone wood cabinetry with curved edges. New flooring in greens and blues was specified to coordinate with wall colors. Privacy curtains were proposed depicting large-scale nature images (such as a tropical beach with palm trees or mountain wildflower meadow with a stream running through). Appropriate CDs accompanied these curtains (i.e. wave sounds or bird song and a babbling brook), all with the hope of creating more peaceful, calming environments.

I held the dream for seven years, during which time I tried to interest these directors in the concept. My family and many special friends stood by me, encouraging me firmly and lovingly, *insisting* that I maintain the feasibility of beginning this program. God had other plans...

He could have let me in on the fact that I would have to be patient during those seven years, move across the country, settle in a new town where I knew no one, and introduce the idea to the Director of Volunteer Services at a local community hospital before the seeds of the program could at last find fertile soil...but I probably wouldn't have believed Him anyway.

In 2007, my husband Ron completed his thirty-year career as a pediatric nephrologist and accepted a new position with a pharmaceutical company near Princeton, NJ. By that time, I had completed thirty years as an interior designer. We moved to Bucks County, PA, that July.

I shared my idea with my new neighbors, who immediately suggested I visit St. Mary Medical Center in Langhorne, PA. They thought that perhaps the Healing Environments Program would be welcomed at this faith-based hospital, home to beautiful Healing Gardens. It was great advice.

In March of 2008, the program was born and continued to grow and flourish for more than nine years. St. Mary, founded by the Sisters of Saint Francis, with their fundamental beliefs of inclusivity and treating the whole person—body, mind, and spirit—this proved the perfect place.

Though I still don't know why Sabah had to suffer, I fully realize that in witnessing his strength, courage, and unfailing resolve throughout this journey, I was given a great gift. The Healing Environments Program evolved from the small seeds of an idea to a fully blooming reality as the direct result of our priceless time together. And by extension, those involved in the program were able to positively impact the lives of many others striving to regain their health or facing their final journey.

My dear Sabah, I am deeply touched to be able to share your story and thus honor your life, your valiant struggle, and your precious memory.

2

Follow Your Dream, Live Your Passion, Fufill Your Purpose

Within each of us is a wellspring of abundance and the seeds of opportunity. For each of us there is a deeply personal dream waiting to be discovered and fulfilled. When we cherish our dream, and then invest love, creative energy, perseverance, and passion in ourselves, we will achieve authentic success.

– Excerpt from *Simple Abundance*,
by Sarah Ban Breathnach, American author

I followed my neighbors' advice and visited St. Mary Medical Center. While enjoying a walk through the main floor corridors, I was greeted by many smiling staff members and volunteers, who asked if I needed help finding my way. I declined, assuring them that I was fine and continued my explorations. As I walked along the main corridor, I came to a beautiful visual display depicting the history of the Sisters of St. Francis. The sisters had founded St. Mary Hospital in the early 1900s in Philadelphia when they nursed the poor of the city during the tuberculosis epidemic. The display was impressive and spanned the entire wall.

[Appendix I - Sisters of St. Francis Photo]

I walked farther and found myself in a hallway where large color photographs of many religious and spiritual sites from around the planet adorned the walls. These included the Golden Buddha, the Dome of the Rock (where Mohamed is believed to have ascended to Heaven), the Western Wall in Jerusalem, the pyramids, and many more. These images spoke volumes to me. The message clearly and beautifully illustrated was, "No matter where you're from, what your heritage or beliefs, we welcome you here."

Healing Gardens

I strolled through the lush Healing Gardens, blooming in their autumn glory, and I saw several patients accompanied by their aides enjoying the sunshine. I remember thinking, *How nice for all of them to be able to take pleasure in being surrounded by nature.* I realized in that moment that I would like very much to work in this hospital. I had no idea if the administration would be interested in the program, but I had to try. I stopped at the volunteer office to inquire about the procedure for becoming a volunteer. I was given an application and submitted it several days later. The form included a section where the applicant could list requests for the type of work preferred. I utilized this space to briefly describe my concept.

Two days later I received a call, inviting me to a meeting to discuss the program in detail. Soon I sat at a conference table with Director of Volunteer Services Lil Schonewolf and then Assistant Director Helen Gordon.

"Joan, can you please tell us more about the Healing Environments concept you wrote of on your volunteer application?"

I detailed the ideas for enlisting the help of off-site crafters to handmake afghans, shawls, and other items of comfort to be offered as gifts to the seriously ill patients at St. Mary. In-house volunteers would be specially trained to visit the patients, deliver these gifts, and spend quality time with them. I also mentioned the other enhancements I had made to Sabah's hospital room. I summed up my comments by saying, "The ultimate goal of the program is to assure these patients dealing with so much stress, anxiety and pain—they are not forgotten, that others who care have the means of helping to ease their suffering."

At this point, Lil and Helen were exchanging glances, smiling, and visually communicating something…but what?

"Would you mind sharing what you're thinking?" I asked.

Lil explained that for quite a while she had felt she was meant to expand the volunteer program, lead it in new directions, and offer inspiring diverse positions to existing and potential volunteers. The problem had always been that she couldn't *see* any specifics…until now. She was very excited by these ideas and the possibilities they presented.

I offered to volunteer my services during the first year to get the program started.

Why did I do this? During those seven years prior to moving to Pennsylvania, I had given a great deal of thought to how to interest hospital administrators in this concept. I also contemplated what *I* needed to do to help it manifest. The answers I received were to remove my expectations of financial reimbursement to help get the program started and to eliminate my ego as much as possible.

Lil introduced the concept to the administrative staff, and we were given approval to initiate the program for a one-year trial. The Community League of St. Mary agreed to provide funding during that trial year, and suddenly, we had the green light.

I took the volunteer training course in November of 2007, and officially started work in January of 2008. One of my initial challenges was that I knew *no one*; I had left all my friends and my fabulous network of interior design and Feng Shui connections acquired during my previous twenty-one years living in Houston. I am forever grateful to the volunteer office staff for providing lists of schools, religious organizations, senior centers, and other local craft groups, as well as retail yarn and craft stores. We sent emails and letters to these contacts introducing our goals for the program, and setting forth our three-fold Mission Statement, developed by Lil, Helen, Wendy (administrative assistant and computer whiz) and me:

Mission Statement

1. *To deliver our message of caring by wrapping our patients in the warmth of handmade afghans, shawls, caps, and other items crocheted, knit, and sewn by individuals and groups throughout our community.*
2. *To offer groups and individuals the rewarding, fulfilling, fun, and purposeful opportunity to reach out to those striving to regain health and well-being, by creating these symbols of caring.*
3. *To teach these skills to the new generation of crafters to help keep these arts alive and thriving.*

The outpouring of generosity from this wonderfully supportive community amazed us all. Our goal of stocking 300 afghans before initiating our patient visits was accomplished by March of 2008.

Three hundred afghans in three months!

Local crafters were thrilled to become a part of supporting our patients. Prior to receiving cabinets in which to store the afghans and shawls, these items were kept in large trash bags in Lil's office. Soon, one entire corner was stacked floor to ceiling with a mountain of black bags. As I walked into her office one morning to add yet another bag to the pile, Lil sat at her desk. I started to apologize for taking up so much of her space.

"Are you kidding, I love it! I show everyone who comes in what the crafters have been able to achieve in three short months. It's a *miracle!*" She was bubbling with excitement and appreciation for the many crafters who had given so much, generously sharing their time, talents, and skills.

But you may wonder, *how did this miracle occur?* We were informed by many crafters that by bringing their afghans to the hospital, they had been able to empty their stash closets filled with blankets they had been making and saving, but not knowing where or to whom they'd be given. They were happy to know the patients would be receiving and using them, *and* excited to clear their closets to have room to make more…and they did.

At my request and with the enthusiastic approval of Oncology Nurse Manager Sondra, we agreed that the program would be introduced on the cancer unit. We all felt this initiative would be a wonderful addition to assist the patients in such a high-stress area. I was so grateful to Sondra, who truly understood the program from the start, and for providing her eighteen-bed unit on which we could begin the trial. I also felt this to be a personal tribute to my Father-in-Love.

Storage cabinets arrived, and we were able to return Lil's office to her. We ordered a wonderful rolling cart, nicknamed the Healing Cart. A lift-up tambour door and large interior enabled our Healing Ambassadors to bring all the handmade items to the unit.

Ribbon that would be used to wrap the afghans and other gifts also arrived. The ivory satin ribbon was imprinted with the message, "Our Volunteers are Special" in St. Mary royal blue. Clear plastic bags were purchased to keep the blankets clean and to enable the patients to see the beautiful patterns and colors of the items. Volunteers, affectionately known as "The Wrappers" worked in my office preparing the gifts for eventual delivery to the patients. No, they didn't perform any *rap music* while *wrapping*.

The Wrappers

The special card designed and attached to these gifts informed the recipients that the item was made by our Hands for Healing or teen crafters. An ecumenical prayer of blessing was also included. As our staff became aware of this blessing card and specifically, the prayer, they kept the cards available on their units. This prayer was read to many patients and their families to comfort and soothe. Washing and care instructions were also printed on the card. (We used only acrylic yarn for ease of care.)

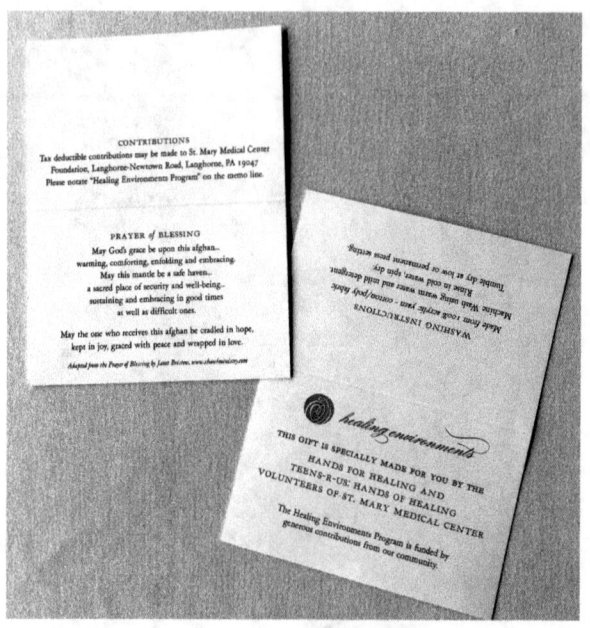

Blessing Card

Prayer of Blessing
May God's grace be upon this afghan…
Warming, comforting, enfolding, and embracing.
May this mantle be a safe haven…
A sacred place of security and well-being…
Sustaining and embracing in good times
As well as difficult ones.
May the one who receives this afghan be cradled in hope,
kept in joy, graced with peace, and wrapped in love.

Adapted with permission from the Prayer of Blessing
by Janet Bristow, www.shawlministry.com

Why afghans, you may ask? One of the Sisters of Saint Francis and talented crochet enthusiast ICU Chaplain Sister Marie Barbara summed up the answer.

"The afghan presented to the patients touches their hearts. As they hold it close and the blessing card is read, they realize it carries our prayers and uplifting thoughts for *them*. These handmade afghans created by the Crafters of St. Mary take on even greater significance when the patient dies. The family receives the blanket and has something tangible to take away with them, perhaps the last thing to have touched their loved one. These handmade items are a symbol of our sincere desire to reach out human to human to express our wish to ease their grief. In this way, we care for each of the patients entrusted to us, body, mind, and spirit, no matter what their beliefs."

Specialized training, conducted by Helen, was provided for volunteers interested in becoming the Healing Ambassadors who would visit the patients. In addition to receiving in-depth hospital-related training, they needed to be willing to visit with seriously ill patients throughout the hospital. They also needed to understand the significance of the handmade items being offered. In fact, several of the Healing Ambassadors also crafted for the program. The trainees were usually outgoing individuals who were able to talk easily with others. We also instructed them in the important art of active listening and the means of encouraging patients to share their feelings.

We began with teams of two visiting the cancer patients with the cart each weekday afternoon and offering the gifts. These warm and friendly volunteers would smile, introduce themselves, state their purpose, and inquire if the patient would like a visit. They endeavored to lighten the patients' moods, joke, and laugh when appropriate, and listen and provide empathy when a more serious demeanor was called for. Occasionally patients weren't feeling up to visitors. Sometimes they didn't want any gifts but appreciated the opportunity to chat with the volunteers and pass the time more pleasantly. (How the visit transpired was always their choice.) The training emphasized the importance of being immediately attuned to the patient's state of mind and responding appropriately and respectfully.

Staying mindful of the fact this was a trial period for the program, we kept detailed statistics logging volunteer hours, items made by crafters and the time needed to complete them, visits made, and how many and which items were given. As the staff throughout the hospital learned of the program, we often received requests for specific items (i.e. neck roll pillows for the patients in Intensive Care and Cardiac Intensive Care Units, and special comfort pillows for mastectomy patients called anti-ouch pillows).

Neck Roll

Anti-Ouch Pillow

To determine patient satisfaction related to the visits, we created a brief questionnaire, and asked for patient or family responses to receive feedback in order to address any issues and improve our efforts. I invite you to read some of their touching comments.

[Appendix II - Samples of Patient Survey Responses]

The trial period was a huge success and the program continued to grow and flourish during the following nine years. New concepts and subspecialties were introduced as we were made aware of needs. The dream became reality.

The stories and experiences that follow were shared by the volunteers, our staff, and our patients. They involve the difficult challenges our patients faced, their worries, feelings, concerns, and how the staff, administrative leadership, the community, and volunteers united to bring about positive change for these patients.

Author's Note:

Names of patients and their family members have been changed to protect their privacy and conform to HIPPA regulations.

3

Vulnerability

God, grant me the serenity to accept the things I cannot change, the courage to change the things I can, and the wisdom to know the difference.

– Karl Paul Reinhold Niebuhr, American theologian, ethicist, and professor

Hospitalized people are often frightened, depressed, anxious, demoralized, and vulnerable. They feel traumatized to find themselves in the strange hospital environment with the necessary, but coldly intimidating equipment surrounding them. It is our responsibility to be sensitive to their fragile state of mind and to offer our willingness to *be* with them at their difficult time, and to assure them they are not alone.

During Sabah's lengthy hospitalization, I was fortunate to be able to take a leave of absence from my interior design practice to be with him daily. I initially felt totally helpless, wanting to bring him comfort, but not knowing what to do. As I left the hospital one night after being with him all that day, I felt completely drained and discouraged. It suddenly occurred to me that despite the wonderful care he was receiving at this state-of-the-art facility provided by the excellent staff, Sabah's beige, lifeless room was sapping our energy. How could he possibly regain his health in such an environment? As his daughter-in-love, I wanted to bring him items that would soothe, reassure, and offer some diversion. As a designer and Feng Shui practitioner, I knew it was vital to introduce color, texture, and natural elements into his surroundings, thereby improving the energy in his hospital room.

I received approval from the staff and went into action; finally, there was *something* I could do. I brought in a soft and colorful afghan that his "Honey" (his loving wife Sylvia) had knit. She had passed two years prior, but I knew that when wrapped in this blanket, he would also be wrapped in her warmth and love.

I brought several family photos of Sabah's "team" and set them on his nightstand facing toward the door. These photos were intended to serve two purposes: he would have his family close, and everyone who entered his room would know this patient had people in his life who cared about him. Many times, I witnessed the staff take the opportunity to have a person-to-person conversation before proceeding with their medical errand.

When they asked about his children and grandchildren, Sabah's face lit with joy. Quite often he sent the visitor off chuckling over something he had shared.

Family

Photograph courtesy of Rita Swinford, RitaSwinford.net

I hung every get-well card he received (and he was a popular guy) to add color and energy to his room, as well as to assure him that many people were thinking of him. Initially, he couldn't hold a book, so I read to him. I also brought in books and music on CD and his Walkman with earphones. When he could finally get out of bed, he needed his orthopedic slippers, robe, and pajamas. Another item that I placed on the mirrored dresser where he could see it was a live orchid plant. Its petals were pure white with deep purple throats. Sabah was a dedicated walker and missed being out in nature, so this plant was intended to bring nature to him. An interesting occurrence was the response of the staff who were captivated by this unexpected addition. As they turned from his bed toward the door, they caught sight of this plant. They stopped, stood very still in front of it, and breathed deeply, drinking in its serenity as they were calmed by its graceful curving branches, beautiful blossoms, and lush green leaves. It struck me that they too were confined within these sterile hospital walls and were also in need of the revitalizing energy that nature and natural images can provide. And this amazing plant bloomed all eleven weeks of his confinement.

The story below illustrates the experience of a man who was dealing with these feelings of anxiety many patients endure. Some people suffer in silence, but occasionally, due to the stress of being in a hospital, the patient may be abrupt or rude. Their response is not directed at the volunteer personally, but thanks to their understanding and ability to ensure a "safe space" for this patient, the Healing Ambassadors helped him open up, express his feelings with crystal clarity, and unburden himself. This chapter includes other stories in which the patients were facing these distressing feelings and the understanding and comfort provided by the volunteers.

*

The Judge

At times our own light goes out and is rekindled by a spark from another person. Each of us has cause to think with deep gratitude of those who have lighted the flame within us.

– Albert Schweitzer, Alsatian theologian, organist, writer, humanitarian, philosopher, and physician

Early one afternoon, Healing Ambassadors Edith and Carol encountered a patient in great distress. During their visit to the oncology unit, they came to a door only slightly ajar. Before entering they checked with the unit clerk to ask about the possibility of visiting this patient. With a slight smile, she said, "Well, you can try, but he's been tossing people out of his room all morning."

These volunteers are two of the kindest, gentlest, and most respectful of women. They both felt strongly that this patient actually *needed* their visit and decided to make a concerted effort to see him.

They tapped lightly on the door and heard a gruff, "What?" They peeked in, introduced themselves, told him they were there for him, and asked if he would like a visit. Another grumbled unintelligible response came from the inner depths, but not a "No, go away."

They slowly pushed the door open and saw this man sitting in total darkness, his head bowed, looking very depressed. They came farther into his room and started speaking quietly, letting him know that it was safe to talk with them, to share his problems and burdens. They invited him to vent his frustrations if he felt like it. Then they stood quietly for a few minutes, letting him take in their words and finally, he began to fill the silence with his emotions.

This man had been a judge for many years. His world had been turned upside down that day with the diagnosis he had received. He was waiting for test results that would determine the course of treatment he would have to undergo. Now he was totally reliant on others and had *no* control. And to add to his aggravation, a baggy hospital gown that hung limply from his shoulders had replaced his tailored suit and judicial robes.

He was so angry he could spit nails! He ultimately confided that his whole identity revolved around his profession; he *was* a judge. What do judges do? They make rulings, pronounce judgements, control their courtrooms, and uphold the law. They are *totally* in charge, and all while wearing their formal judicial attire. No wonder he was infuriated and despondent. And a person doesn't have to be a judge to experience these feelings.

When a situation like this presents itself to our Healing Ambassadors, and it's evident that one volunteer needs to stay with the patient and continue the conversation, the other teammate carries on with visits to the remaining patients on the unit. Edith stayed and asked if she could pull a chair close to his bed.

His reply was a gruff, "Okay."

Volunteers are specially trained to practice "active listening," which entails leaning slightly toward the patient with a pleasant countenance, while giving their *complete and undivided attention.* With gentle prompting, Edith was able to invite him to express his anxiety (loudly at times), and release some of his anger while feeling secure. When she asked if he had family who would be visiting, he said yes, but not until that evening. He admitted he was also experiencing intense feelings of isolation. Edith assured him again that she would stay with him as long as he'd like.

He finally felt comfortable enough to share some stories related to his work as a lawyer and judge and expressed the intense fear that his diagnosis would put an end to his career, which had brought so much meaning and fulfillment to his life.

By this time, Carol had returned, and as it became clear the judge was tiring, they said their farewells. He graciously thanked them both for their time and understanding.

Edith and Carol weren't able to bring the judge joy that day, but as he eventually felt more comfortable releasing his feelings, they *were* able to alleviate some of his tension, help him to calm down, get some rest… and he stopped tossing people out of his room.

As Edith and Carol passed the unit clerk's desk, she looked up in amazement and asked how they had managed to speak with him.

"We offered to truly listen to his concerns and accorded him the same respect and dignity *we* would want to receive if we were in his position."

*

Just A T-Shirt

For it is in giving that we receive.

– Saint Francis of Assisi,
Italian Catholic friar, deacon, and preacher

Director of the Spiritual Care Department, Jack Geracci, shared a story about one of the chaplain students who was working with a patient about to be discharged. The shirt he had been wearing when he was admitted had been damaged. A staff member offered to give him one of the hospital gowns to wear home. He refused the offer, saying that wearing the gown outside would make him feel humiliated. He would rather leave with no shirt than wear the gown.

The student went to the volunteer office to ask if they had another alternative. They did. He provided the patient a new royal blue St. Mary T-shirt, a gift, to wear home. The patient put it on and said, "Now I feel human!"

While caring for people in desperate situations we, the caregivers, need to employ as much creativity as we possibly can. Providing some semblance of normalcy and comfort is vital.

*

Popcorn

The world is hugged by the faithful arms of volunteers.

– Terri Guillemets, American quotation anthologist
…and sometimes by "Secret Bears" …

On my rounds, I stopped at the room where Ed was sitting in his recliner. I asked if he would like a visit and when he said yes, I wheeled in the cart. After introducing myself and telling him I had gifts to offer him, we started chatting. He wasn't really interested in any gifts, but it seemed he needed to talk.

Ed confided to me that he was facing surgery the following day and was understandably stressed. He wanted to be strong for his family, and in any event, they wouldn't be able to get to the hospital until later that evening (they were all at work) and he was extremely anxious. I said, "Well, I'm here right now and if you'd like, we can visit for a while." When I asked if I could sit down, he consented. Bringing us to the same eye level helped him relax and he was able to speak of some concerns and gradually unburdened himself.

As we sat there, I noticed that rather than a hospital gown, Ed was wearing a white T-shirt and flannel lounging pants in the distinctive Scottish Black Watch tartan pattern of blue, black, and green plaid. We had recently been given a donation of twelve-inch bears (a good size for adults as well as children). Some of our seamstresses had made clothes for them. One of the bears had white fur and a vivid green vest. I offered Ed this "Secret Bear" and smiling quizzically, he took it. They looked like a perfect pair sitting in the recliner together and a smile bloomed across Ed's face.

I explained that these are special bears, that he could tell his bear any secret or problem, and the bear wouldn't tell anyone. I further explained that we only ask two things of the recipient: one, that he give the bear a name, and two, lots of hugs. Usually, the patients needed some time to think about this, but when I asked Ed if he had a name, he immediately said, "Yup, he's going to be Popcorn."

I asked, "Why Popcorn?"

He explained, "My daughter has a white poodle named Popcorn, and this bear reminds me of her."

He and Popcorn looked so comfortable together as I left shortly after. I don't know if Ed shared any secrets with his new pal, but I could see that he was visibly more relaxed. I would love to have heard the conversation with his daughter and family that evening when he told them about *his* Popcorn.

*

Little Hands

Please, Mom and Dad…my hands are small.
Don't expect the bed I made or the picture I draw
to be perfect—just love me for trying.

– Excerpts from *Please Mom and Dad*, by
J.L. Richardson, American author

Our youngest crafters were from a church Sunday school class of two-, three-, and four-year-old children whose teachers were helping them learn about God's love by making tiny teddies about eight inches high. The children's tiny fingers were ideal for tucking the stuffing into the bears' arms, legs, and tummies. Each bear had a pocket sewn to its tummy that held a copy of the letter printed below. The children made these bears specifically to help other children in the hospital who were frightened and perhaps in pain.

Attn: Volunteer Department:

The enclosed Teddy Bears are a gift from the 2-, 3-, and 4-year-old Sunday school class at Emilie United Methodist Church, Levittown, PA. Over the past year, one of the topics we have been reviewing with the children is how God's love is always with us. We also worked on a service project so that we could give back and help show God's love. The children helped stuff and seal (press the Velcro strips closed) the enclosed Teddy Bears with the intent to donate them to the children's ER. This way, if there is a child who needs treatment and does not have something to hold on to, they could be given one of these bears and know that he/she is not alone, that God is with them and loves them. Each child in the class also kept a similar bear. Each time they hold it, they can remember that not only is God with them, but that they were able to help show God's love to someone else. We hope that this will help those receiving it through a difficult time.

Thank you in advance for your consideration and assistance in handing them out as you deem appropriate.

With God's Love,
The Students and Teachers of the 2-, 3-, and 4-year-old Sunday School Class

The Pediatric ER nurses were *thrilled* with the bears and many children benefitted from these thoughtful gifts. They were especially helpful when the young patients needed to receive an injection or experience something frightening. The nurses were able to distract and soothe their young patients with these special gifts.

The crafters also had fun making cheerful blankets for our young patients.

Small Bears

*

A Grateful Recipient

Volunteers are love in motion.

– Author Unknown

Joyce was diagnosed with invasive lobular breast cancer in 2014. She had been making afghans for the patients at St. Mary for several years and had always enjoyed the work. However, her crocheting had to be put on hold when her surgeon told her she would require a lumpectomy. When the surgeon actually performed the operation, four more tumors were found that had not shown on the original mammogram, and those were removed as well.

After her recuperation from that first procedure, she and her doctor had a follow-up consultation during which they decided together that a mastectomy was the best course of action, since the surgeon couldn't be absolutely sure she had gotten every cancer cell. Three weeks later, Joyce returned to St. Mary for further surgery. She was in the hospital that day and part of next (which happened to be her birthday). She was feeling very low, when a volunteer entered her room holding a beautiful pink-and-white afghan and also a small (anti-ouch) comfort pillow to use where her breast and some lymph nodes had been removed. She was very touched. It had never occurred to her that she would be on the receiving end of the program.

Pink and White Afghan

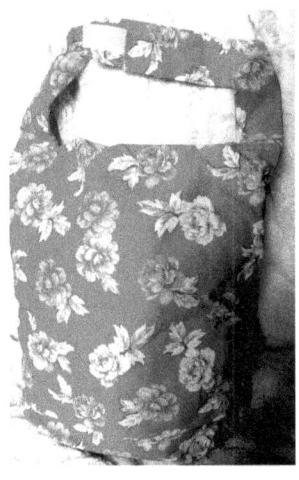

Anti-Ouch Pillow

In her letter of appreciation to us, she said, "I know that love and prayers went into every stitch of those gifts, and I appreciated them so much. I use my little pillow every night in bed, and it helps relieve the discomfort. The lovely afghan has a permanent home in my living room. I thank all the crafters for their hard work and hope this program will continue. As both a participant and recipient, I can vouch for how essential it is for both the creator and receiver. It brings comfort and blessings to all concerned. I am so deeply thankful."

Harry went through some very trying experiences following his discharge. He would require pinpoint laser radiation, but first he had to be prepared. To be certain the radiology technicians were able to accurately target the same precise location with the laser beam each time, a red line tattoo was drawn at his jaw and along his neck. He was also fitted with what I called an "iron mask," a stainless-steel halo that would hold his head still during treatments. The framework was so heavy that metal shoulder supports were required to disperse the weight. The halo was tightened to his scalp with bolts. This apparatus looked to me like an instrument of torture from the Dark Ages, rather than equipment essential to the administration of state-of-the-art laser therapy in 2000.

Sabah was absolutely calm throughout the procedure as the halo and shoulder supports were adjusted.

I, on the other hand, was *seething*. When we got back home that first day, he went upstairs to rest, while I ran to my bedroom crying, asking why such a sweet, kind, wonderful person had to be put through such torture. I grabbed the spiral notebook and pen that I always kept next to my bed to capture my thoughts, ideas, and dreams. I *had* to release this anger!

I clutched the notebook, grasped the pen as if it were a dagger, and scribbled on the page, digging into the surface of the paper. Then I viciously tore it out, crumpled it as hard as I could in my hands, and threw it with all my might across the room. Tears streamed down my face as I repeated this action over and over until I fell back on the bed totally exhausted.

During the time of his treatments, side effects, and diminishing strength, I received no answers to my question. All I could do was be there with him and for him.

4

What To Talk About? How To Listen?

The real art of conversation is not only to say the right thing at the right place, but to leave unsaid the wrong thing at a tempting moment.

– Lady Dorothy Fanny Nevill, English writer, hostess, horticulturalist, and plant collector

Concerns regarding what to talk about might run through your mind when contemplating visiting a friend or loved one in the hospital or other health facility. In fact, some people have confided that they felt so uneasy about this, it prevented them from visiting at all. Being with a friend who is suffering is not easy. Sometimes just sitting together quietly, perhaps holding hands, maybe with your eyes closed in loving silence can transmit your message of compassion. Playing soft music can also help fill the void.

When I was with my Father-in-Love, going to or waiting at appointments, we could always chat about the grandchildren and their latest activities. Another favorite topic was our beloved Boston sports teams.

If the one you're planning to visit has specific interests, such as sports, gardening, cooking, music, crafting, whatever, it helps you both if you come prepared to discuss those interests. Our ubiquitous cell phones and access to the internet keep a world of information at our fingertips and ready to be discovered.

The stories that follow offer some practical suggestions and ideas to solve this dilemma and help to make the experience more pleasant for all concerned. They also provide practical suggestions for what to say…and what *not* to say.

*

Chatty Cathy

Listening is active. At its most basic level, it's about focus, paying attention.

– Simon Sinek, English author

After asking the unit clerk if there were any patients who might need special attention, we were directed to Cathy. We were told Cathy didn't have many visitors, and also wasn't very talkative.

Volunteer Sylvia had the uncanny ability to help people to open up and start talking. She walked up to Cathy's recliner, introduced herself and me, then said, "We're just stopping by to see if you'd like a visit today." It appeared Cathy might decline, but Sylvia barreled on telling her about our new Respite Visitor program.

Walking into a patient's room with her disarming smile could usually get a conversation going. Then saying, "We're here for *you* today. Is there anything you'd like to talk about?" Asking open-ended questions and then pausing, giving the patient time to answer, to fill the silence, usually proved to be a good way to invite them to fill the void. One of the key aspects of our training was to help the trainees become comfortable with that silence and to wait patiently.

As the silence filled the room and Sylvia and I stood expectantly, Cathy finally replied, "Well, once I get talking, I'm a real 'Chatty Cathy.'"

Sylvia's smile spread across her face as she promptly responded, "And I'm a real 'Chatty Sylvia!' Is that a Philly accent, Cathy?" Cathy confirmed it was, and Sylvia said, "Me too!"

And they were off. They talked about their neighborhoods, shops, landmarks, and favorite restaurants. They soon discovered both had been teachers. Cathy's life revolved around her students and passion for teaching. An engaging twenty-minute conversation followed.

It is so common for us to ask, "How are you?" when we meet normally. This is *not* a question to ask a patient. How would they be? They're in the hospital, not well enough to leave. A better alternative is to ask how their day has been so far. It's a good idea to bring a newspaper or some other reading material, even though many people bring their cell phones and tablets with them to the hospital now. If you plan to stay a while, a deck of cards can help pass the time. Bringing some items that create a sense of normalcy is very helpful.

*

The Power of Listening

Be still and know that I am God.

– Psalm 46:10

When Chaplain Madeline arrived on the unit, she heard about the "difficult patient" who was causing quite a stir among the medical team. She braced herself for what might be a challenging visit. The patient was a ninety-year-old man of Jewish faith. He could barely walk, was frail, and suffered with heart disease. As he began to share some of his life story, it was obvious to Madeline that this retired psychologist was very intelligent, articulate, and had voiced some legitimate concerns.

He just wanted someone to *listen* to him and to validate his experiences. From employees of a home health agency, he had suffered several experiences of abuse. He claimed the agency workers would come to his home, ignore him, do very little, and not provide the care he expected and required.

"I am considered an old man who just complains," he told her. He hired a lawyer to investigate his accusations, but to that point there had been no resolution. She assured him the social worker assigned by the hospital to his case would send a caring team of home health workers to his home. If there was any mistreatment it would immediately be reported to the Area Agency on Aging.

As he expressed his feelings of anger and resentment, he began to talk about his wonderful marriage of sixty years and how he missed his wife. They adopted a son who has mental challenges, but this special child had brought a great deal of happiness into their lives. He continues to provide for his son and was very eager to return home to check on him. The man spoke so lovingly about his family that she thought to herself, *Is this the cranky old man who is dismissed by so many?* After they talked for some time, a smile spread across his face, and he didn't seem as tense.

Madeline asked if she could pray for him and his son. He began to cry as the words of familiar psalms were read. He said he missed going to synagogue due to his ill health and inability to drive or travel about. He had to rely on the kindness of a few friends who occasionally called or stopped in.

They finished their prayers and she promised to visit with him again soon. As she walked away, she realized that underneath the rough exterior, there was a kind, compassionate, generous, loving husband and father, a man who had accomplished a great deal of good in his life. Those moments spent with him helped her appreciate the true power of a smile, a prayer, and a listening ear.

*

Life Story Writers

Words are sacred. They deserve respect. If you get the right ones, in the right order, you can nudge the world a little.

– Sir Tom Stoppard, Czech-born British playwright and screenwriter OM, CBE, FRSL

When I was going through the experiences with my Father-in-Love, I kept a journal to record our days and to release my troubled feelings, as well as to note positive and happy times we shared. I found it helpful to be able to get those thoughts out of my head and down on paper. I wish I had also recorded stories Sabah shared with us in his own voice. He would tell us about his youth growing up in Dorchester, Massachusetts, a suburb of Boston, populated mostly by Jewish working-class families at that time. He told of his mother who cared tenderly for his sister and him, of his father the butcher with the beautiful tenor voice. He told us of the day he saw Savtah riding her bike past his house with her friend, how their eyes met, and he felt a jolt. (He was later to learn she had felt it too.)

But I would love to have recorded these stories and have them captured in his own voice with his strong New England accent. If you can relate to this concept, don't wait to record your loved one or friend. People often enjoy being asked about their younger years, or about their happiest memory.

In 2012, we introduced the Life Story Writers program at the hospital to capture important aspects of our patients' lives. We held discussions as we considered the possibility of introducing this concept and how best to bring it to our patients. It was decided that we should enlist the nurses' help in selecting patients feeling well enough to be interviewed on one unit where they remained for three to seven days. Our intention was to honor the patients, but also to help our staff get to know their patients as the *individuals they were beyond the hospital walls.*

We reached out to our community, requesting people with writing backgrounds as well as those interested in creating the visual story boards that would illustrate aspects of the patients' lives. The volunteers underwent extensive training, including sharing some details of their own lives and creating their own story board. Role playing was conducted in groups of three. One trainee would act as the patient being interviewed, and one would ask questions of the "patient," while the third performed the duties of scribe, taking detailed notes.

The stories below illustrate that when this program worked, it was very meaningful for the patients, volunteers, and staff. However, it proved to be challenging in the hospital setting. It soon became obvious that the patients who were kept longer were usually too ill to be interviewed. And many of the other patients were discharged too quickly for us to be able to conduct the interview, compile and write the story, return to the patient to confirm its accuracy, and print out the finished copies (for the patient, their family, and for the patient's file). Then, based on the information shared by the patient, at least another day or two was required to create their story board.

Author's Note:

We came to the realization that this worthwhile program would be better suited to a nursing home, senior day care, extended care, or hospice facility. But as you are reading this book, perhaps you're thinking of someone you'd like to sit with and learn more about. Our ubiquitous cell phones make it easy to record and video the person's life details spoken in their own voice. Being able to see and hear our loved one takes on special significance after this person has passed.

Once the Life Story Team was introduced to a patient who was interested in being interviewed and the consent form was signed, we could begin the process. We started by asking them to tell us several things they would like people to know about them. But if you're wanting to interview a grandparent for instance, you might ask them what life was like when they were a child (yes, like back in the "old days" before color TVs, remote controls, cell phones, and the internet) and use your cell phone to record their voices. We discovered people loved to share stories about their lives. To have someone actually *listen* to their stories was an unexpected gift to them.

*

My Journey Thus Far

The best way to find yourself is to lose yourself in the service of others.

– Mahatma Gandhi, Indian lawyer, anti-colonial nationalist, and political ethicist

Bobby K was frequently a patient at St. Mary in 2013, beginning in early January. When originally given his diagnosis, he was told by his physicians he had four to six weeks to live and was advised to get his affairs in order. It became vital to him that he heal wounds within his family, to learn and study, and to make peace with his God.

He gladly consented to permit one of our Life Story teams to interview him six months after his original diagnosis. He provided wonderfully detailed information, which enabled us to write his story and create his life story board.

When asked what four things were most important to him that he would like others to know, he responded with the following:

(1) Information and knowledge are keys to forming meaningful relationships, with God and my fellow man.

(2) I am in the process of studying the roots of Christianity with the desire to expand and deepen my relationship with God.

(3) I am constantly challenging myself, researching and listening to different beliefs to improve myself and to understand others better. I research to be able to make informed decisions about who I am and to determine my core beliefs.

(4) Open communication, research, and study are the tools I use as I seek the truth, and work to develop relationships built on mutual respect.

Bobby K's Board (in progress)

Bobby K was born in Braddock, Pennsylvania, in 1946, the oldest of six children. His father worked for US Steel; his mother was a homemaker. His father was abusive to all the family, which left deep scars and damaged the interfamily relationships. Bobby was never able to reconcile with him but has forgiven him. He is close to his mom and also his sister Mariana who live in Florida, as well as his daughter Nadine in New Mexico. He has two grandchildren.

He attended the College of Santa Fe where he majored in political theory. Since becoming ill last January, he has used this time to delve deeply into his beliefs. Bobby wasn't expected to pull through at that time, and as he lay in the hospital, he realized that he wasn't afraid to die, but he was afraid of dying out of grace with God. He focused intently on creating a more meaningful relationship with God. As a child of God, he believed he shared God's DNA and would be reunited with Him in Heaven. He also believed he and his earthly father would reunite and he looked forward to that time.

With the gift of this time, Bobby studied various religions and planned to explore the Koran, as well as the history of the age when it was written in the hopes of better understanding the Muslims of today.

He also memorized various prayers and psalms with the intention to become a psalmist. He studied the prayers of St. Mary, Zachariah, St. Stephen, St. Peter, the Song of Solomon, and the Book of Psalms, having been led by Spirit and his heart.

As we interviewed Bobby, he mentioned wanting to start his own blog with focus on political theory and current events. He planned to apply his knowledge of past political theorists such as Plato, Aristotle, Socrates, Algernon Sydney, John Locke, Henry David Thoreau,

Gandhi, and Martin Luther King Jr., and combining the thinking of current political experts to assure the information would be relevant and interesting.

Bobby had many heroes in his life, people whose lives and beliefs he admired. For instance, Roberto Clemente was not only a great right fielder for the Pittsburgh Pirates earning twelve Gold Gloves, but a man who truly made a positive difference in the lives of those in need. He headed relief efforts in Puerto Rico after a massive earthquake hit Nicaragua in later December 1972.

Author's Note:

Bobby K passed away within two weeks of this interview. We felt so fortunate to have had the opportunity to get to know him. We were able to give him a copy of this interview and his life story board was displayed prominently in his hospital room on the oncology unit until his passing. Following Bobby's death, his story board was taken to his funeral, where family and friends learned many things about him that they had never known. His family kindly decided the board should be donated to the hospital where Bobby could continue to reach out and be an inspiration for others.

*

"The Brits"

Courage is what it takes to stand up and speak; courage is also what it takes to sit down and listen.

– Sir Winston Churchill, British politician, army officer,
writer, and Prime Minister of the UK,
1940-1945 and 1951-1955

Daphne was a seventy-five-year-old lady who was suffering with lung cancer. She was from London and had fallen in love with her American soldier husband when they were both young. He brought her to the states, where they raised their family and were married fifty-four years.

When volunteers Evelyn and Wendy (aka "The Brits") entered her room at St. Mary to conduct a life story interview, they were all delighted to discover their mutual British roots and experience a "touch of home." Their interview flowed beautifully, and a lovely bond was formed. She and her mum invited the volunteers to their home for tea following Daphne's discharge. Wendy and Evelyn happily accepted.

The date was set for the following week, and when they arrived, they were escorted into a beautifully decorated living room. English bone china statuary, furniture covered with brightly patterned floral fabrics, and intricately detailed hooked rugs met their eyes. Lacy white curtains fluttered at the windows.

Tea was served from an elegant tea service decorated with pink rose buds. Finger sandwiches, scones, and biscuits (cookies) were plentifully served on platters. The ladies enjoyed reminiscing about growing up in England and sharing stories of their lives in America.

Unfortunately, Daphne's cancer was advanced by that time, and she died at home two weeks later. However, she and "The Brits" were able to enjoy some "luvely" time together.

*

"Sunny"

What sunshine is to flowers smiles are to humanity.

– Joseph Addison, English author

Sonia loved this program because it afforded her the opportunity to help patients "go" to a happier place. She had a delightful way of putting people at ease and communicating her caring. With the lilt of India in her voice, she always approached them in a gentle manner. And with a smile curving her lips, she would say, "I just stopped by to see if you'd like a visit today."

If they consented, asking them if they would share three things important to them which they would like others to know, helped shift their focus away from their medical concerns. It also opened a wide vista of topics she could use to move the conversation forward, to expand these discussions.

Sonia vividly remembered her interview with Mary Ellen (aka "Sunny"). She said that everyone who came into her room called her the "Smiley Face Lady." That fact stayed with Sonia, because Sunny was truly bubbly, despite being a patient. A Philly girl, she loved to cook and bake, sew, and spend quality time with her children and eight grandchildren. Her husband was an army helicopter pilot, so Sonia included the US Army insignia and picture of a helicopter on Sunny's story board. They had lived in many states as he was transferred to various bases. She had always felt her essence, her purpose, was to share her smile with as many people as possible.

"It gave me such joy to be able to go back to the volunteer office to start Sunny's board. Using my hands and some simple materials I created a board that expressed who "Sunny" truly was. I made a border with smiley face stickers and a large smiley at the top."

Magazine pictures of young children, families, and baked goods filled much of the space. Images of her dancing with her husband in her pretty blue satin dress with white polka-dots at their wedding and across the country, Alaska and Hawaii provided the major focal point. Toward the end of their interview, Mary Ellen confided, "Life wasn't always easy, but we did love to kick up our heels whenever we had the chance!"

Unfortunately, by the time the board was complete the next day, Sunny had been transferred to the St. Mary Physical Therapy Hospital across the street. However, one of the volunteers was going there that afternoon and delivered it. "Sunny" was overjoyed and as she wept through her smile, she said she would always treasure Sonia's gift. And Sonia received a gift also.

"I felt so happy to be able to make her something that would touch her so deeply. That shared joy touched me too, reached down through my layers to my core and brought a quiet satisfaction to my soul."

Sunny's Board

One of our patients facing death who agreed to be interviewed was finally able to speak of horrors he had witnessed as a soldier during World War II. He had kept these stories to himself for many years. The willingness of the volunteers to listen finally persuaded him to share what he had never even told his wife or children about these experiences, feeling he always wanted to be strong for them.

Volunteers are often perceived by the patients as "safe." It is frequently easier to speak of difficult things to a stranger rather than with family members. With gentle encouragement from our Life Story Writers, this veteran was able to release these memories at last. During the years since the war, he had been suffering with what we term today as Post Traumatic Stress Disorder and had lived a tortured existence as a result. He carried tremendous guilt that *he* had survived when so many of his comrades had been slain. Finally, he was able to let go, lay down this terrible burden, and die in peace.

5

Joy Amidst the Sorrow

Life is an opportunity to contribute love in your own way.

– *Love, Medicine & Miracles* by Bernie Siegel, MD,
American author, retired pediatric surgeon

Despite all the suffering we see in the hospital, there are moments of pure joy as well. Many of these experiences were brought about by the wonderful staff members going above and beyond after hearing of a special situation or need. When a loved one is a patient in a healthcare facility, options for creating an atmosphere of happiness or positivity may seem limited. It definitely requires some thought to go beyond the obvious.

While spending precious time with my Father-in-Love during his final months, we found meaningful ways to enjoy life, despite all he was experiencing. He appreciated old movies, especially westerns, reruns of comedy television shows, and watching all the Boston sporting events. He deeply loved phone calls with his children and five grandchildren who at that time were spread all over the country. He received calls and cards daily from friends and clientele from his store, which helped him stay mindful he was not forgotten.

I hope the following stories help you or someone you care about find meaningful ways to enjoy life, despite current challenges and difficulties.

*

Rainbows Everywhere

I shall pass through this life but once. Any good thing therefore that I can do or any kindness that I can show to any human being, let me do it now. Let me not defer it or neglect it, for I shall not pass this way again.

– Henry Drummond, Scottish evangelist,
biologist, writer, and lecturer

Many of the patients I tried to visit one morning were out of their rooms or sleeping. But finally, I came to a room where a patient was lying in the bed. A woman whom I was to learn was his wife was sitting quietly close by. I stepped in and smiled as I told them briefly why I was there. The patient, Jack, looked cold and had the white hospital blanket pulled all the way up to his chin. I told him I had handmade afghans on the Healing Cart made as gifts by the Hands for Healing Crafters in our community, and he was welcome to choose one. I said, "I see that you're tall, and I have three that are quite large right now." (His feet were pressed tightly up against the footboard. I later learned he was 7'6" tall!) I put the large ones on top of the cart so that he could easily see them.

He looked closely at the blankets and then at his wife. It was clear she was very emotional, and though I wondered why, I kept my focus on Jack. As he looked at her, he gently said, "It should be the rainbow one, right Honey?"

She nodded and I could see she was close to tears and fumbling for a tissue. I placed the box within easy reach as she nodded her thanks.

I felt terrible that in some way my visit was triggering such a strong response. Nevertheless, I proceeded to open the afghan and lay it over Jack. It covered him completely and he held it closely. We gathered around his bed and joined hands while I read the blanket blessing. The tears were now streaming down his wife's face, and I asked if they would *please* explain the significance of the rainbow to me.

Jack again looked at his sobbing wife and gently asked, "Shall I tell it, Honey?"

She again nodded her assent. It seems his mother-in-law, Linda, had collected rainbows for many years. Friends and family loved to give her rainbows in every medium—ceramic, photos, calendars; she had collected hundreds of images of rainbows, which she displayed throughout her home. Linda had passed several years prior, but every time any family member sees a rainbow they always say, "Hi Mom!" believing she is saying "Hi," letting them know she's ok and sending her love. I thanked them both so much for sharing their story, wished Jack well, and completed my visit, leaving some magazines and activity books to help them pass the time.

What I would like to share with you at this point is that I had crocheted this afghan, but it could have been made by any of the crafters. Not only had I made it, but I was *inspired* to do so from its beginning. In the craft store, while trying to decide on the yarn I would purchase for my next project, I saw all these beautiful bright rainbow colors and thought it would be fun to use them all. I felt the vivid colors would bring a patient some cheer. Also, in Feng Shui teaching, each color represents energy and when all the colors are present, the energy in the space is balanced.

As I worked on the blanket, the thought occurred to me that our patients come in all sizes, so why not make this one extra-long for a tall person? Were these ideas really Linda working from beyond inspiring me, as her way of reaching out to her "long, tall, son-in-law?" The night before this visit, I realized I had been working on this blanket quite a while and was ready to finish, wash it, and bring it to the hospital. I have to wonder at the synchronicity.

I stopped by their room the next day, but Jack had been discharged. I was happy for him, but disappointed to miss the opportunity to visit with them again. I knew I would be writing this book at some point and would have loved to ask for a picture of the blanket. Due to HIPPA privacy regulations, there was no way I could get in touch with him.

Fast forward five years...

My Wednesday Healing Ambassadors were just returning to my office from their visit to the units. They started telling me about the wonderful experience they had just had with a gentleman and his son. The man was telling them about the rainbow afghan he had received while a patient five years prior. I immediately asked, "Is he really, *really* tall?" When the response was an emphatic *yes*, I asked what room he was in and dashed upstairs. There was Jack, totally filling the bed head to toe. It was so exciting to be reunited with him and to meet his equally tall son (7'7"). He said he had been well; he was at St. Mary for something minor.

He told me how much he and his wife had been enjoying the afghan, especially on cold nights. And when it's not at the foot of their bed, it has a "place of honor" draped over a chair in their bedroom. I was pleased and truly touched that one of my afghans had such a positive impact. Then he looked at me seriously and said, "Joan, I want you to know that if, for any reason, we had to leave our home quickly, that afghan would be one of the treasures we would take with us!"

Rainbows Everywhere

To any crafters reading this who might think they're "just making" an afghan, scarf, shawl, neck roll pillow, whatever, think again. You are creating a gift that is going to touch a life, whether for your family, a friend, or for someone you will never meet; you are doing work that many people cannot do and you're using your skills and abilities to reach out to others with compassion, to provide comfort. You are doing important work.

And just a parting thought: when you get those nudges, hunches, inspirations…listen. I'm pretty sure these nudges were sent from Linda, telling me in her most effective way this afghan was intended for her family as her means of communicating her love and concern during their difficult time.

Author's Note:

Other "events" took place on various units throughout the hospital, including weddings and birthday celebrations. One of the most touching was the *seventieth* wedding anniversary celebration for a couple in their nineties. The staff ordered cake, hung streamers, and served sparkling grape juice. Both were patients at St. Mary at the time. She was on the oncology unit and close to death. But to see her eyes light with happy tears, love, and joy when the staff wheeled her husband into her room, was beautiful and heart-wrenching. As staff from both units sang "Happy Anniversary," many eyes were moist witnessing the powerful bond of their love.

*

Casino Night

*Whatever you vividly desire, sincerely believe, and
enthusiastically act upon…must inevitably come to pass!*

– Paul J. Meyer, founder of Success Motivation Institute

Doris lay near death on the oncology unit. Her husband, Frank, had been with her constantly, but on that
day, he became very agitated. The nurses were concerned and asked if there was *anything* they could do
for him.

He finally broke down and explained that he was
facing the fact that he would not be able to keep a
promise he had made to his wife. Doris loved to go to
Las Vegas casinos. When they had received the news
that she had stage four cancer, he promised to take her
back one more time. However, her cancer progressed
much more rapidly than anyone had anticipated, and
here they were in the hospital. The nurses listened
attentively as an idea was beginning to formulate; a
way they could help this couple. The idea was to transform Doris's room into a "casino".

The next day they went into action. Twinkle lights
were hung around the room. Some of the off-duty
nurses came in dressed in black slacks, white shirts

with red cummerbunds, and bow ties. A slot machine was rented, and refreshments of sparkling grape juice and light snacks were set out. Decks of cards and play money were everywhere.

The overhead lights were dimmed, and the twinkle lights sparkled as Frank woke his sleeping wife. Her eyes lit up and a wan smile spread across her pale face! She played the slot machine one more time and beamed at her husband and the staff as she said, "You did it, you brought Vegas to me!"

Doris passed away two days later, cradled in her husband's arms. Despite losing her, Frank was content knowing he had been able to keep his final promise, thanks to the caring staff willing to go above and beyond.

*

Shopping…in the Hospital?

Save time in your day for spontaneous occurrences!

– Anonymous

We were warmly greeted with smiles from Sharon and her sister as we entered Sharon's room. After introducing ourselves, we told her that we had gifts to offer. We showed her the afghans, dignity robes, hats, scarves, and other items on the cart. Her smile became even bigger, her eyes got bright, and as she looked at her sister, they both burst out laughing! While continuing to giggle, she explained why they found this situation so humorous.

In her family, she has the title of "professional shopper." When she and the extended family take trips together, the others go to museums, sporting events, enjoy hiking, golfing, skiing, or engage in other activities. Sharon is in charge of shopping. Prior to the trip, she researches the best shopping in the area; specialty items and products the location is known for…wine, leather goods, art, etc. She puts together the shopping itinerary for all who want to join.

We began to chuckle, and she got very excited looking at all the beautiful handmade items. When I told her about the program and the "Army of Crafters" numbering over 300, who donated their time to create these gifts, she became intrigued. For these sisters, each item took on special meaning and they were both impressed and very appreciative.

Then, I could see a subtle change come over Sharon, as she "got down to the serious business of shopping." She had a discerning eye, and as she looked over everything, she chose some lovely items. She popped a hat on her head, selected a matching scarf, and added a neck roll pillow in the same pastel colors. We offered her the hand mirror always kept on the cart, and she grinned again as she admired her selections.

She then looked at her sister, and once more burst out laughing. Turning back to us she said, "My husband is *not* going to believe this! To think I can be a hospital patient, and still keep shopping…I can't wait to see his face when he walks in and sees my new acquisitions…and what great bargains!"

Scarves & Hats

*

Her Unique Chaplaincy in the ICU

Through our handwork, God has engaged us in the great act of compassion. Our handwork is weaving us—our hearts and souls—into the truth of God's love.

– *Knitting into the Mystery,* Susan S. Izard, American author and co-founder of The Prayer Shawl Ministry [Appendix III]

Sister Marie Barbara is the Intensive Care Unit (ICU) Chaplain at St. Mary and a member of the Order of St. Francis. Her patients are very ill and sometimes close to death. She is also a very talented crafter, creating unusual afghans into which she has intentionally woven prayers and blessings. She is in the unique position to not only *create* the afghans, but also to occasionally *give* them to the patients with her personal blessings and expressions of comfort.

Sr. Barbara's Afghan

When I spoke with her, I asked if she tells the recipients she made it or if she gives her creations anonymously? She said that when she makes an afghan, weaving in those prayers, blessings, and love, this aspect holds special significance for her, but she usually gives it anonymously. Occasionally, she knows the patient and/or their family. Then the gift becomes personal and it's appropriate to tell them she made it.

Sister Barbara actually taught her mother to crochet, so they had a special bond through their handwork. During her mother's treatment for cancer, her ability to continue to crochet provided her some level of contentment and purpose. During this difficult time, Sister Barbara's mother used what little energy she had to make each one of her children an afghan.

Sister Barbara was taught to crochet by one of the sisters in her order. This nun tried to teach Sister Barbara one way to hold the hook, but she wasn't getting it. When shown another way, she was able to move forward.

"When I was teaching my mother," she said, "we had just the opposite issue. The afghan my mother made for me was a ripple stitch pattern in shades of blue, green, and yellow. I still have it in my room. When I wrap it around myself, I can still feel her tenderness. These blankets last forever."

This activity has brought so much pleasure to Sister Barbara's life that when she learned of the Healing Environments Program starting at St. Mary, she felt it would be a lovely way to share this pleasure. She enjoys this creative work in the evening while relaxing. It also provides a unique way for her to touch the lives of the seriously ill patients admitted to the ICU, over and above her work as the chaplain. When she spreads a blanket over the patient and those in the room gather around the bed as she reads the blessing card, the words "cradled in hope and wrapped in love" take on special significance.

"It touches me deeply when I present afghans to the patients and their families. Despite all they're going through, they are overwhelmingly joyful. I try to ask the patients what their favorite color is. When they receive 'their afghan' in 'their color,' they are thrilled."

Sometimes she doesn't have the chance to ask about color, and she goes to the afghan cabinet in the volunteer office to see what's available. Quite often, when she brings it back to the patient, one of the family members will call out, "That's her favorite color! How did you know?" It seems God guided her hand.

Sister Barbara's participation in this program brings deep feelings of joy and grace. In the presence of a patient who is end stage (near death), the family is understandably distraught with their grief. By bringing this symbol of love and caring, an item totally unexpected in a hospital setting, let alone in an ICU, they are often moved to tears. Often the family asks if they can pay for it, but she responds, "This is a gift. It's made especially with our patients in mind with prayers and blessings woven into each stitch."

Then she tells them about the many crafters who diligently work in their homes, crocheting, knitting, or sewing these beautiful, one-of-a-kind items. Not that they know the patients personally, but they carefully make each item lovingly by hand, knowing it will be given to someone in need of their special message of caring and comfort.

"Their thoughts are with you, and they want you to know you and your loved one are not forgotten." With tears glistening in their eyes or on their cheeks, the families gratefully receive these gifts.

The ICU team loves this program. In addition to the afghans to warm their patients, the staff deeply appreciates the hand-sewn neck roll pillows. Not only do these pillows provide comfort, but they also serve a vital function when a patient is intubated or has a tracheotomy. In these cases, it is imperative to keep the patient's head and neck supported so that the airways remain open. The neck roll pillows are the perfect solution.

The staff always tries to have plenty of both items on hand, but occasionally, when they run out, they know a call to the volunteer office will ensure quick delivery of these essential supplies by the red-jacketed volunteers. The volunteers, whether working on-site or from home, are vital to helping the ICU team fulfill their service to their patients to the very best of their ability.

Sister Barbara once had a very interesting experience in a patient's room. The female patient was sleeping most of the time. Her husband was at her bedside constantly. Sister Barbara entered the room and asked him if she could bring his wife an afghan. He said yes, so Sister Barbara asked what color she might prefer. Just at that moment, the patient became lucid and very distinctly said, "Pink." Sister went to the volunteer office and fortunately found a lovely afghan in multiple shades of pink. And as the icing on the cake, there was also a beautiful neck roll pillow in a pattern of pink roses. As she brought them to the patient, the woman's eyes lit up and a beautiful heartfelt smile spread over her face. Her husband was all smiles too.

On another occasion, a female patient was lying close to death in the emergency room. Sister Barbara entered and started speaking softly to the family. Eventually she told them about the afghans available for the patients and asked what the woman's favorite color was. Her husband responded, "Mary loves periwinkle blue."

This is not a color readily available, and Sister Barbara realized that, but as she opened the afghan cabinet, she knew God had been at work again as she found a beautiful afghan in this color. She hurried back to the ER clutching her precious find. As the family gathered around Mary's bed forming a prayer circle, Sister Barbara spread the blanket over her and read the blessing. With tears in his eyes, Mary's husband thanked Sister Barbara and told her he would cherish this afghan forever.

"Some people might think, 'But it's just an afghan, a pillow, or a shawl.' However, it's clear by the responses of those who receive them, these items hold deep and lasting significance."

*

A Gentle Way of Touching Souls

Let no one come to you without leaving better and happier.
These are living expressions of God's kindness: kindness in your
face, kindness in your eyes, kindness in your smile.

– Mother Teresa Bojaxhiu of Calcutta, Roman Catholic
Nun, and Founder of The Missionaries of Charity

A cheerful smile, a warm hug, help finding your way, comfort at the bedside of a dying patient, Sister Mary Ann could and did deliver all of these. She was *everywhere* in the hospital, spreading compassion and sunshine. She attended those in great distress in the ER, sat quietly as she listened to final words or wishes, held a hand, there to comfort the family when a loved one died tragically and suddenly, whether at the bedside or in the morgue.

I am blessed to have known her and to have had her in my life. When I arrived at the hospital the day of my meeting with Lil and Helen, she was the greeter at the front entrance, the first person I met. She took my chilly hand in her warm one and with her lovely, kind smile, asked, "What brings you to St. Mary today?" Helen was standing close by, and I was able to read her name tag. I told Sister Mary Ann that I was there to meet with Helen and Lil. She pulled me into a hug and whispered in my ear, "They have to watch out for us little ones, don't they?" (We're both about five feet tall). Her words amazed me because only Lil and Helen had any idea why I was there. I drew back to look directly into her eyes, wondering just what she knew or intuited. As I came to know this dear soul better, I understood that she had many abilities and gifts, great wisdom, and insight among them.

I was also fortunate that Sister Mary Ann was my mentor during my first bedside No One Dies Alone vigil. She introduced us both to the patient, Anne, and led me through all the preparations, speaking softly. Anne was being kept comfortable via a morphine drip and was lying still in her bed. The lights had already been dimmed, but we lit some battery-operated votives to shed a pleasant glow, brought our Psalm and prayer books, and as the patient was Catholic, Sister chanted her rosary frequently. She gently stroked Anne's arm and murmured softly to her. She continued to assure Anne we were with her, as Sister shared her special brand of loving kindness. As the evening stretched on, Sister and I spoke softly, prayed, and recited blessings together. Gradually, Anne's breathing became more irregular, and with each of us holding her hands, she passed peacefully.

*

One More Day to Sew

I'd rather sew than eat!

– Betty F, Gail and Wilma's mom, amazing friend,
wonderfully talented seamstress, American Sewing Guild
Chapter Leader, generous, warm, kind,
and thoughtful human being.

Sometimes a memory gets etched into our minds so vividly, it's like a movie clip. It might last a minute, a few hours, a day, or longer. I am fortunate to have such a memory of an afternoon shared with Gail. Although we didn't know it at the time, it would be her last day to sew. She had been a patient on the oncology unit at St. Mary for more than a week, and on several occasions had been close to death. The volunteers visited regularly, but often found her asleep.

On this day as I entered her room, I was amazed to see her propped up in bed hand sewing a neck roll pillow. Her mother Betty had brought a stack that needed to be filled and the openings needed to be sewn closed. An entire circle of crafters filled the room, each working on a pillow, chatting, and happily enjoying their time together. Gail's sister Wilma joined us when she arrived after work. I pulled in another chair, and we sat together laughing and sharing stories as we worked. Gail finished one pillow and started on another. She was positively jolly, as she conversed with everyone. We were all thrilled to see her so animated.

Gail passed away peacefully the next day. When I was able to speak with her mom the following week, Betty expressed her gratitude for that last day.

"Gail had such a great time visiting with everyone. Wilma and I are so happy she had one more day to sew, to do what she loved the most and to share it with us and so many dear friends."

Neck Roll Pillow (Veteran)

*

Rockin' to Heaven

Embrace your individuality. Love what you love without worrying about judgement.

– Egypt – The Goodvibe Co.

Jamie was a patient on the oncology unit where her friend, Sondra, was the nurse manager. Jamie had stage four cancer and lay close to death. Sondra checked on her frequently throughout the day, but usually found her friend sleeping. At about 10:00 that evening she went to her room again, and found Jamie, her jaw tightened, eyes squeezed shut, and her hands clenched into fists. Thinking she was in pain, Sondra hurried to her bedside and asked what she could do to help. Jamie's response was, "Could you *please* turn off that #&x*# elevator music?" Sondra immediately turned it off and asked if there was some other music she'd rather listen to, knowing we had an extensive collection of CDs in the Healing Environments office. Jamie quickly responded, "Yea, how about some Led Zeppelin?"

Sondra knew we did *not* have hard rock music in our library, but she sprang into action. She called her daughter at home and asked her to retrieve her CD collection from the attic along with her headphones and bring them to the hospital ASAP. By 11:00, Jamie was plugged in and turned on, her eyes closed in bliss, her toes and fingers tapping to her favorite tunes, her head swaying in time with the music.

Jamie passed at about 2:00 a.m., rockin' her way to Heaven!

This story is an excellent lesson to remind us of the fact that we're all different and unique. We are charged to honor and respect the patients' wishes whenever possible. What one person may think is wonderful, may be pure torture for another. Even though my Father-in-Love was in a private room at MD Anderson, he always played his music through his headphones so he wouldn't inadvertently disturb anyone.

Love of music provided a favorite avenue for elevating or lightening Harry's moods. He appreciated all kinds of music—big band, Broadway musicals, classical, jazz, and popular hits. Invariably after listening to showtunes, he would be humming selections for weeks. He and Ron played cards in the evenings, and I could hear them laughing from the other end of the house. Although it wasn't easy, Harry was amazingly adept at maintaining a positive state of mind, and I'm certain *gratitude was the key*. I vividly recall him expressing his sincere thanks for even the smallest things. Though the cancer had invaded his brain cells, he was determined not to let it steal all enjoyment from his final days.

6

Crafting with a Purpose

I'm convinced that crochet (and knitting) is witch's black magic…My wife does that stuff. She sits there with two 'magic wands,' performing complex movements, while chanting and cursing, looking at a spell book…and then…blanket!

– Quote from Cheeky Witch

*

What it Takes to be a Crafter

What is required to become a volunteer crafter? Simply the desire to do something creative to provide comfort for someone going through tough times. For instance, making a fleece blanket doesn't require the ability to sew, knit, crochet, or weave; sharp scissors, a ruler, and a flat surface will suffice. A class of third graders was able to make ten blankets for the patients as their community service project several years ago, and third and fourth grade Scouts have also made many for our patients.

[Appendix III – Hand-tyed fleece blanket instruction video available on YouTube]

The items that have been described for the Healing Environments Program were made with the intention to provide comfort in many different forms. For example, mastectomy pillows provide pain relief and support immediately following breast surgery. Many of these patients report they sleep with these pillows for years afterward. They are also used as protection from seatbelt pressure. Afghans, quilts, shawls, and capelets were taken home, enjoyed constantly, displayed in a place of honor, and shown to friends and family.

Crafters of all ages working from home to provide thousands of items for the patients (as well as for others in need) were the "heroes behind the scenes," helping to keep the Comfort Cart filled with their amazing creations. They generously shared their time, talents, and abilities, the knowledge and experience gained in their lives and a desire to be purposeful as they gave to others.

Crafting can also be a wonderful social outlet. Many of the crafters who knit, crocheted, and stitched for us also belonged to other groups. We held monthly craft meetings at the hospital, but other groups had weekly gatherings, which provided opportunities to form friendships and share common interests. Especially after losing a spouse, retiring, or moving to a new location, it can be difficult to form a new community. Crafting can provide an avenue to connection.

Every fall and spring, we held craft sales to raise funds to support the program. Because the items made for this purpose were intended to be sold instead of given to patients, the crafters could go "outside the box" with the items they made. This fact provided them freedom to explore and expand the types of creations and materials used. It was fun for all to see the clever ideas proposed, whether or not others chose to make them. Many of the staff attended the sales and would sometimes commission a crafter to make specific items (such as winter scarves) in particular colors as Christmas gifts for their family or friends. And those of us who worked the sales had a marvelous time together and made great memories. One such experience occurred when one of the staff was admiring the "fuzzy scarves" we had made. Initially, she tried to decide which ones to buy, but at last gleefully said, "I'll take 'em all." (All twelve!)

What follows is a collection of experiences collected from crafters involved in the program. Some were still challenging themselves with new patterns in their seventies and eighties, keeping their minds sharp and hands busy.

*

Mastering the Ripple Stitch

*It doesn't matter if you try and try and try again and fail.
It does matter if you try and fail and fail to try again.*

— Charles Kettering, American inventor,
engineer, and businessman

"Perseverance Pays Off" could also be the title of this story. For years, Terry had tried repeatedly to learn the very popular crochet pattern known as the Ripple Stitch. Her sister had shown her the process many times, but when Terry attempted it on her own, the sides would grow diagonally outward. She was discouraged and would revert to doing the Granny Stitch.

Terry was also my wonderful volunteer administrative assistant. One of her primary responsibilities, in addition to compiling all relative statistics, was to record all the items the crafters working at home had made and details pertaining to each. Since the crafters' work was done off-site, it was also extremely important that their volunteer hours be accurately recorded and acknowledged. Volunteers annually receive "Hour Pins" in recognition of their cumulative hours contributed to the hospital. Her work was a vital part of our statistical analysis, especially during the initial trial period. We wanted to be able to accurately record the progress. As we worked closely together, Terry and I became friends.

One Tuesday, as we were working in the office, she confided her frustration with the Ripple Stitch. I had seen a pattern for this stitch in our collection just the previous day that utilized two strands of yarn held together. There are two specific benefits of this technique, the first being that you have more yarn to hold as you're beginning the design, the second, that you use a larger crochet hook, which creates larger stitches that can easily be seen and accurately counted.

At the end of her shift, we sat together so that I could help her get started. The larger stitches proved to be a major benefit for Terry, and she was able to keep track of the number of stitches easily. She was so excited the following week when she brought her work in and proudly displayed her progress. Even now, I'm not sure if she were happier about finally eliminating a source of constant frustration, or by the fact that her sister wouldn't be able to call her a "Ripple Stitch Dropout" anymore. Don't we just *love* our siblings' teasing?

Soon Terry was thrilled to be able to complete entire afghans. One day, while visiting patients, a gentleman selected one of Terry's blankets in the beautiful autumn colors of forest green, rust, brown, and gold. As I spread it over him, he commented, "My wife crochets and tries to make this pattern, but she can't get

the stitches right. They zig and zag all over the place."
We invited her to come in for a lesson in how to *master*
the Ripple Stitch.

Terry's Ripple Stitch

*

"Monsters" and Other Creations

*With all my heart problems, God has given me life for a
reason. When I'm making something from my heart and soul,
honoring the creative gifts with which God has blessed me,
that's powerful. But then when I give it away to someone I
know, who needs this message of caring, that's everything! It's
all about giving of ourselves, sharing our gifts, reaching out to
express God's love. When I'm serving others, I'm serving God.*

(These were Peg's opening words to me
at her volunteer interview.)

– Peg H., American artist, seamstress, poet, philanthropist,
retired Registered Nurse

Peg has experienced a lifetime living with illness. She
has chosen to make very unique items for others who
are suffering.

"I purposely create these cancer monsters to look
strange, because that's exactly how people can feel
when they are struck with this disease. They feel 'off' as
if their bodies are betraying them. These patients often
experience intense feelings of isolation." Some of her
monsters had three eyes, were bald, or had strange tufts
instead of hair. Her intent was to give patients something tangible to hold, perhaps project their feelings
onto, and help them know they're *not* alone.

Peg's "Monsters"

The Newborn Nursery staff struggles to bring solace to grieving parents whose babies die. Peg's answer was to create "Comfort Cards" that were attached to the crafters' Baby Bereavement Items. The staff presented these to the patients as they were discharged.

Peg's Baby Cards

Preemie Blanket & Cap
Blanket is 12"x12", Cap is 2 ½"x 3"

Peg also contributes to animal shelters. She creates doggie jackets made from salvaged sweaters found at local thrift stores. She cuts off the sleeves from sweaters destined to be discarded. Peg doesn't waste anything!

As a former nurse and visiting nurse, and now as a volunteer, the *seemingly* small items she makes for people struggling with life's most serious issues let them know they are being thought of. Her personal intent is to deliver the message, "We care about you, we pray for you, you don't have to face this alone!" These gifts can light up their eyes and make their day. These people are human beings, and as such deserve respect and understanding.

When she cared for patients at their homes as a visiting nurse, they sometimes felt so solitary. She encouraged their neighbors and their doctors to come to the patient's home. Peg always tried to help them create a network to stay connected and also to discover their options, what was available through community services and outreach.

Peg has the amazing ability to help people discover and value their gifts. Sometimes people will see what she's making and say, "Oh, I can't do that; I can't make anything." Well, maybe that's true, but she encourages them to discover that there are many other things they *can* do. An example of this concept was illustrated when Peg brought a piece of military fleece to her friend Ruth who had many health problems and was feeling down. Peg had cut the strips on the four sides and patiently showed Ruth how to double knot the strips to complete the blanket. Ruth discovered she really enjoyed doing the work, so Peg started bringing the fleece to her by the bagful. When completed, Peg laundered them and brought them to the volunteer office ready for delivery to the veterans. With the realization that, thanks to the work of *her* hands, a veteran would be warmed and comforted, Ruth came to appreciate a renewed sense of purpose and self-worth.

One of Peg's friends, a veteran, was near death. She went to visit him and presented him with one of the fleece blankets. You'd have thought he'd been given pure gold. As he clutched his beautiful blanket, covered with images of the Stars and Stripes, he felt so honored, humbly grateful to be acknowledged for his service by this gift. Every time she visited him, that blanket was covering him, in his lap, or around his shoulders.

As a member of the American Sewing Guild, Peg teaches sewing skills and other crafts to the next generation of crafters. One ASG member's granddaughter is a Girl Scout. Peg suggested that the troop make the fleece veteran blankets as their community service project. The Scouts gladly took on the project. Fifteen veterans received these beautiful warm blankets along with the Scouts' handwritten and illustrated cards thanking them for their service to our country.

LIFE

L is for LIVING every day to the fullest!

I is for being INDEPENDENT; not letting anyone else run or ruin your life!

F is for FINDING new ways to learn, live, love, grow every day of your life...to regenerate, renew, re-experience, recycle, re-create yourself!

E is for EVERY BLESSING starting with this very moment! Waking up this morning...taking your next breath...hearing and feeling your heartbeat...hearing a baby cry or a child laugh...feeling the human touch...feeling your tears running down your face then tasting the saltiness...Can you ever remember it being so quiet you could hear the snow fall softly to the ground? And what of the beauty of that new fallen snow? Remember your first kiss or gentle hug? What of the sound of the water rolling up on the shore as you watch an awesome sunset? – Peg H.

Enjoy your life. It is yours. We only go around once, so make the most of it. Share your gifts, talents, and love. It will always come back to you at some time or place that most surprises you.

*

Passionate About Sewing

The key to realizing a dream is to focus not on success but on significance—then even the small steps and the little victories along your path will take on greater meaning.

– Oprah Winfrey, American media executive, author, and philanthropist

Betty was the leader of a local chapter of the American Sewing Guild for four years, 2009-2012. ASG, a national organization over 30,000 strong, is composed of people who love to sew. Some chapters have committed time each week to making items of comfort which they donate. Betty's chapter is known as the CHCS—Creative Hands in Community Service. The patients of St. Mary have been the fortunate recipients of many of the items this chapter has sewn.

- **Face Masks, and Protective Gowns** – Newly added during the COVID pandemic. These items were sent to caregivers on the front lines, wherever they might be. Many of the ASG members nation-wide have set aside current projects to make millions of these desperately needed items.

Their creative efforts for the patients included:

Dignity Robes – worn by cancer patients as they receive radiation treatments

Hair-loss Caps and Kerchiefs – (for those who have lost hair due to radiation)

Heart Pockets – sewn onto the corner of afghans into which the blessing card is inserted

Neck Roll Pillows – for general comfort and to support patients' necks

Bedside Pocket Pouches – which hold glasses, cell phones, computer tablets, nurses' call button/ TV control within easy reach

Lap Activity Pads – used for physical therapy teaching, Alzheimer, and dementia patients, and those who have suffered brain damage due to disease or accident

Reading Glasses and Eyeglass Cases – protect donated glasses

Wheelchair and Walker Bags – attached to these devices to keep needed items conveniently close

Sewn Eyeglass Case

Every time a new item was suggested to us by the nurses, the volunteers, or by the group themselves, they always said, "Yes, we'll make those too!" During her four years in the leadership position, 4,070 items were sewn, and the members contributed 5,076 hours making those items.

Bill Brown became the leader in 2013 and has been fondly referred to as "The Head Rooster" of the CHCS (pronounced Chicks) group ever since. (No one can accuse crafters of lacking a sense of humor.) Bill is retired but you'd never know it from the hours he devotes to sewing. When asked how/when he started sewing, he responded that his mother was a seamstress, but she was much too busy to sew the sock puppets and items he needed to practice his work as a magician, so he taught himself. He made the sock puppets and conducted puppet shows in his back yard for friends in the summer. He started learning magic tricks and eventually became a professional magician. But he sewed the special cloths, sleeve alterations, and even a "dove pocket" where the live bird could be safely concealed until being revealed.

ASG conducted annual Sew-ins every fall at St. Mary. The members arrived in the morning with their sewing machines, set up, and created about thirty-five of the lap activity pads and over sixty neck roll pillows for our patients. Bill spent about 100 hours prior to these events preparing the individual pieces that the members sewed onto the lap pads during the day.

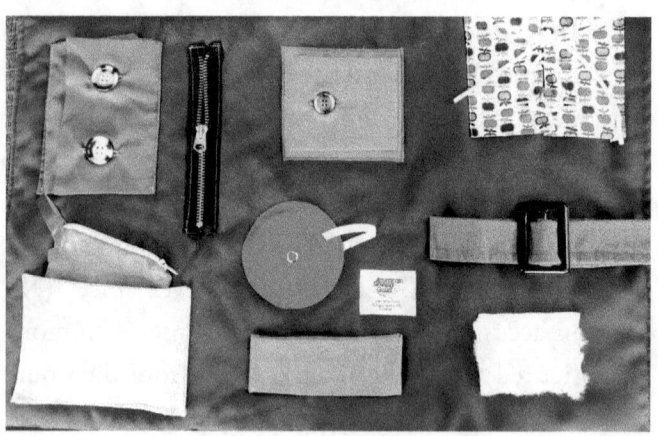

Lap Activity Pad

As you can see from the photo, these items are very detailed, but if you're a patient who has suffered an injury, has had a stroke, or is struggling with dementia or Alzheimer's disease, these activity pads provide the means to help therapists re-teach patients important skills such as buttoning, zipping, putting items into a pocket, tying shoelaces, etc.

When I asked Bill what other projects the group is involved with, he shared a wonderful story about a global movement that distributes sustainable menstrual health solutions to women and girls in developing countries. "Days for Girls" was founded in 2008 by Celeste Mergens.

Utilizing small pieces of cotton or cotton flannel (5"x5"), the members create sanitary pads for these girls in packages of two. The countries where these items are brought are so hot that the girls can wash them, hang them on a tree, and they dry in twenty to thirty minutes. Without these items, girls are unable to leave their dwellings during their monthly cycle. This equates to them missing school during this time *each month* (Appendix III).

The latest development with this program is that sewing machines, fabric, and detailed classes instructing the girls themselves how to make the pads are being provided. The pads last from three to five years. Each kit contains reusable cloth menstrual pads, panties, a washcloth, soap, and zip-closure plastic bags, all in a draw-string pouch. During the time this program has existed, over one million kits have been distributed.

Whether it's an item of comfort for their local hospital or making these important items that travel halfway around the world, the members of the American Sewing Guild are finding ways to put their sewing skills to work every day.

*

God's Caring Stitchers

When you wholeheartedly adopt a 'with all your heart'
attitude and go all out with the positive principle,
you can do incredible things.

– Norman Vincent Peale, American Protestant clergyman,
author, and speaker

Cindy has been the leader of her knitting and crochet group since 2000. Her devoted Caring Stitchers make beautiful knit lap robes using three or four different colors of yarn and a variety of stitches. They then contribute these afghans to St. Mary as well as to area shelters for the homeless. The group also makes baby items for single mothers and women's shelters, small children's toys for the Shoebox Ministry (Appendix III), as well as other local and international programs.

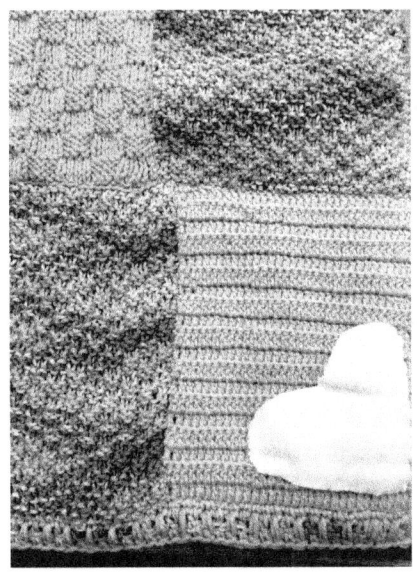

Cindy's Blanket with Heart

After working for sixteen years to build her crafting group, she now has over thirty dedicated members. They enjoy coming together in fellowship at the Lutheran Church of God's Love in Newtown, Pennsylvania. During COVID the members have continued their work from home. They combine their skills to create handmade items for those in need. Rather than ask one crafter to create a whole afghan, they started sewing the "Warm Up America Foundation" squares (Appendix III) and put them together, thus creating a whole afghan. From these squares the group obtained many of the intricate patterns they still use in their lap robes today. These small squares are easily transportable, which enables the crafters to work on them in the car, while waiting in the doctor or dentist office, anywhere.

Three knitters are given three different coordinating colors and they choose whatever pattern they want to use in making their squares. When the squares are complete, they are collected and sewn together to make a complete afghan. An edging is added in one of the colors to form the finished border. Like the spokes on a wheel, each person is vital to the completion of the whole.

A special blessing ceremony is performed in the church sanctuary three times a year. The lap robes (and any other crafted items) are displayed along the altar for all to see. The purpose of the blessing ceremony is three-fold: 1) to bless the creations made by the crafters, as well as those who ultimately receive them; 2) to enable the church members who have been financially supporting the group to see the products created utilizing their funds; and 3) to enable the crafters to see how their squares have been utilized to form beautiful complete afghans ready to be given to someone in special need of their unique gift. These lap robes are the gifts contributed to the patients at St. Mary Medical Center.

Cindy continued, "Our ministry hasn't stopped there. God is orchestrating an amazing journey for us.

Over the years, I have been fascinated to witness how people are drawn to our program. Quite often, when we have a specific need, the perfect person 'shows up' who can fulfill that need. Each person is unique and brings new ideas, suggestions, and energy to the group. A Jewish lady came to the door of our crafting room one day and said, 'I'm Jewish, can I join your group?' We all said sure! She said, 'I only make chemo (hair-loss) caps; is that ok?' "That day, our chemo cap production began, Cindy proudly stated. These lovely colorful caps made with soft baby yarns are taken to the Joan Karnell Supportive Care Program at Abramson Cancer Center in Philly to help their cancer patients who have suffered hair loss during their treatment."

Several years ago, another new member mentioned the Prayer Shawl Ministry by Susan S. Jorgensen and Susan S. Izard in their book, *Knitting into the Mystery*. The yarn required for their patterns was outside the group's budget, so the idea was tabled. Two years later, the idea was mentioned again. This time, however, a donation of the necessary yarn "showed up" several weeks later. So…their prayer shawl ministry began. The church gives these prayer shawls to members of their congregation in need of comfort and healing. Others were sent with their youth group when they traveled to New Orleans to help the victims of Hurricane Katrina.

"We are blessed by the donations of yarn we receive. We make our items for patients with 100 percent acrylic yarn to provide ease of care and to guard against possible allergies to wool, Cindy explained. However, at one point, we had received quite a bit of lovely wool yarn. I put the word out to the crafters again asking for suggestions regarding what we should make with the yarn. Someone mentioned the program called 'On Eagle's Wings' in the Northwest Territories in Canada, which our church already supported. Our beautiful hand-knit wool sweaters now wing their way on the 'Wings' plane, along with other much-needed articles and the word of God to these remote areas of Canada. It seems there are no boundaries to our ministry!" (Appendix III).

They've developed a solution for the issue that arises with the small balls of leftover yarn that has become very popular—"Prayer Squares" or "Blessings in your Pockets." These gifts begin as a 2.5" x 2.5" yarn square either crocheted or knit. A Bible verse is printed on paper in a 2"x2" format, laminated, and cut to size. A hole is made in an upper corner of the paper and is then placed over the yarn square. The two parts are then tied together with yarn and can be easily tucked into a pocket or purse. When Cindy first proposed making these for their congregation prior to Lent, her pastor loved the idea. When Cindy asked how many would be needed, and he said, "Oh, about 300-350," she swallowed her surprise, but silently wondered how they would *ever* accomplish this task in time.

Now why would I not trust that this goal could be achieved? Cindy thought later.

These pocket-sized gifts are given to the homeless in their breakfast bags as well as to the patients at St. Mary and to the chaplains who distribute them.

Sadly, several members of their group have passed over the years. The group felt the desire to do something special to honor their memories. The family of the deceased crafter typically receives a prayer shawl from the church when their loved one passes. But the members decided to make an afghan to honor the crafter. Once made, a photo was taken of the blanket and was sent along to the family with a card in which Cindy expressed the group's appreciation for the crafter's contributions and mentioned the organization that received the afghan.

"Our Caring Stitchers group is such a blessing, said Cindy. Many friendships have developed that extend outside the group. People who are lonely or struggling in some way have friends to call upon. The group is intergenerational and so much can be learned from the wise elders of our group who are still vital, energetic, and full of inspirational ideas. Many years ago, a knit and crochet group for the youth of our congregation was formed. It was beautiful to see the seniors teaching the next generation, and everyone benefitting."

Cindy and I reminisced about the fall craft sales she and her amazing husband Norm participated in to help raise funds for the Healing Environments Program. I had memories of the two of them lugging plastic bins filled to the brim with all the items intended for the sale. Cindy had the amazing skill of displaying everything beautifully. A vivid memory popped into my head, and I said, "Oh, Cindy, remember when Norm helped put together those shelves that weighed a TON?" We had a great laugh about that. Cindy's husband has been at her side throughout all the years of her crafting group, supplying manpower, ideas, his computer guru skills...anything and everything she needed.

Cindy's final thought to share with everyone was, "If you have a passion, but perhaps you can't see the whole concept, be patient and 'stay tuned.' It may be 'out there' perhaps in a slightly different form, or maybe it needs to be approached in a subtly altered way, but don't give up. Keep showing up, talking with people about it, and at some point, the vision will be clearly revealed. The members of God's Caring Stitchers of God's Love Lutheran Church send you blessings as you go forward on your journey."

*

The Power of the Blanket

Gratitude unlocks the fullness of life. It turns what we have into enough and more. It turns denial into acceptance, chaos to order, confusion to clarity.

– Melody Beattie, American author

A young man suffered a severe heart attack and was brought to St. Mary. While in the hospital, he was visited by the Healing Ambassadors who invited him to choose a blanket from the Healing Cart. Later when his mother came to visit, he said, "Mom, can you believe someone crocheted this afghan and gave it to me? I feel like I'm wrapped in love."

Unfortunately, this young man died, but to honor her son, his mom became one of our Hands for Healing crafters, making beautiful quilts and other comfort items for patients. She was working on a patriotic quilt when her son was sick. Though painful for her to continue, she completed it and donated it in his memory.

"As a mother and fellow crafter, I want you to know what a wonderful and deeply important service you provide."

*

Teaching Her Passion

Give a man a fish, and he'll eat for a day; teach a man to fish, and he'll feed himself for the rest of his life.

– Chinese Buddhist Proverb

As a breast cancer survivor herself, Rose found visiting the patients on the oncology unit especially meaningful and felt an immediate affinity with them. She had learned to knit when she was twelve, taught by her Aunt Jen, who created beautiful knit outfits for Rose and her younger twin sisters when they were little.

Rose was one of the Healing Ambassadors and during a visit she and I entered the room of a young woman, Liz, whom we could see was feeling very depressed. As we showed her the handmade items on the cart, she chose an afghan in soft shades of moss green, perfect with her green eyes and auburn hair. As she wrapped it around her shoulders, she was transformed. Her face lit with a smile and those green eyes sparkled. The program impressed her so much that she expressed her interest in learning to knit. She wanted to be able to make a sweater for her new puppy and make things for other patients.

Rose immediately offered to teach her the basics of knitting. Of course, we didn't have the supplies on the cart, but I quickly went back to our office and brought everything they needed to get started. In the meantime, Rose kept Liz company, chatting about the program and the patient's excitement about learning to knit…even while being in the hospital.

When I returned, Rose sat with her and spent some time showing her the basics. I can still see them sitting together with the knitting needles and yarn. For Liz, her day and her attitude were totally transformed. Her depression vanished to be replaced by feelings of purpose and the intention to learn a new skill. Did it take her mind off her problems? Absolutely. Rose left her smiling and sincerely grateful.

Rose's spirits were lifted as well by sharing the gift of her knitting skill with another. "This work is what gives my life purpose and meaning. Being a participant in this program has made a huge positive impact on my life."

Our Healing Environments crafters have varied widely in age. You were introduced to the two-to four-year-old children in the Pre-K Sunday school group. Our most senior member, Helen, was still creating beautiful, crocheted items in her 100th year. Many ordinary people like you and me of every age in between participated. Age is definitely not a factor in determining our ability to do good work; it only takes the desire.

We received artwork from elementary school students throughout the community. These creations were laminated and offered to patients to help brighten and personalize their rooms. Their images of rainbows, ice cream cones, kites, hot air balloons, and animals brought many smiles to the patients' faces. One husband told us that due to his wife's frequent in-patient visits, they had received three of these creations. With a twinkle in his eyes and a grin he told us, "We're using them at home as cheerful placemats. Three more and we'll have a full set of six."

Lil and I spoke with the students and teacher of a local third-grade class who planned to make fleece blankets for the patients. We talked with the students about what makes *them* feel better when they're sick. Answers of "chicken soup, my favorite bear (or other stuffed animal), my favorite pajamas" were mentioned. But quite a few said, "My blanket." For the patients in the hospital, it's the same.

The students' willingness to make the blankets and give them to the hospital was a wonderful act of kindness. It also instilled in these young minds, the community mindedness we are fortunate to enjoy in our area.

One of our devoted volunteers, Ann K, is still tying fleece blankets at her assisted living residence at the ripe young age of 98! They are then distributed by Carol Fenton, the founder and leader of the local craft group known as "Connect-the-DOTS". These lovingly made blankets go to the newborn intensive care patients at Jefferson Hospital, the veterans at St Mary Medical Center, as well as other recipients.

Ann K, 98 years young, with just a few of the fleece blankets made with love for those in need

Fleece "Mountain"

7

Many Ways to Make a Difference

*We must not, in trying to think about how we can make a
big difference, ignore the small daily differences we can make
which, over time, add up to big differences
that we often cannot foresee.*

– Marian Wright Edelman, American activist for children's
rights and author

It certainly isn't necessary to be a crafter to enjoy the
myriad volunteer opportunities. Though the volunteer positions discussed here were implemented in
the hospital setting to benefit patients, families, and
staff, you may choose to research opportunities else-
where. In this chapter, Healing Ambassadors, Challah
Delivery volunteers, as well as Respite and Veteran
Appreciation volunteers relate their tales as they served

on the front lines in the hospital. Your unique specialties and experiences could benefit others in diverse and beautiful ways.

Healing Ambassador Teams

*

"The Kathys"

Every day is a good day to have a good day!

– Cathy and Kathy, Healing Ambassadors

One aspect of the Healing Ambassador teams that always fascinated me was the synchronicity of the partnerships created. "The Kathys" or is that "The Cathies?" had been Healing Ambassadors for four years, long enough to know they *loved it.* They also enjoyed a special bond thanks to their names.

"Even when it appeared the patient might decline a visit, we still introduced ourselves, said Kathy. 'Hi, I'm Cathy with a C.' 'And I'm Kathy with a K.' For some unknown reason, the patients and their visitors found this hysterical, and we got them laughing. Before we knew it, everyone's spirits were lifted!"

They were fresh faces, visiting in a pleasant way to help take the patients' minds off the medical issues that had brought them to the hospital. Their intent was always to bring comfort, to chat about whatever was on the patients' minds, and to hopefully leave them in a better place mentally and emotionally. They brought the clear and powerful message that beyond the excellent medical care provided at St. Mary, the patients were cared for by the volunteers.

By offering each patient the handmade gifts on the cart, they also shared the crafters' intentions to assure these patients they were not forgotten. On many occasions Kathy witnessed the dramatic change of expression on the patient's face when they came bearing gifts.

Cathy added, "They just can't believe it and their faces go from disbelief and awe to wide smiles and often happy tears. We always felt so grateful for our own good health that enabled us to visit these patients who were facing so many difficulties."

One patient who was visited by "The Kathys" gave them this delightful compliment:

"The Kathys were like spark plugs; they energized my hospital room with their lively conversation and beautiful gifts. I felt supercharged after their visit!"

*

Do You Have Anything in Blue?

We can complain because rose bushes have thorns or rejoice because thorn bushes have roses.

–Abraham Lincoln, American statesman, lawyer, and sixteenth president of the United States

Carol and Edith, Healing Ambassadors for more than six years, were an amazing team. During that time, they worked together to bring comfort, cheer, understanding, and the gift of their time visiting with the oncology patients. They had also enjoyed some wonderful experiences.

One day they entered the room of an elderly woman whose grandson was with her. When they introduced themselves and explained their purpose, the young man informed them his grandmother didn't speak English, but he would gladly translate for her.

They opened the cart to display the gifts and told the young man his grandmother could select an afghan if she'd like. He patiently explained and helped her do so. Carol also mentioned the blanket included a blessing, and she asked if they would like her to read it. He nodded and as Carol read each line, this devoted grandson translated the words into Spanish. They could see from the small smile that spread across her face that his grandmother understood and appreciated the message.

What was also evident from the pleased expression on the grandson's face was that *he* was happy to have been able to help his grandmother in this small way. As she gathered the afghan around her frail body, she smiled sweetly at Edith and Carol. The volunteers knew she would be a bit more comfortable while staying warm wrapped in this symbol of caring. And thanks to her grandson, she also clearly understood the good intentions embodied in it.

Edith told of another unusual visit when a patient *sang* to them! "He had to be about ninety years old with a warm smile that lit his face and crinkled the skin around his eyes, revealing a hint of mischief, despite his situation. We didn't recognize the lyrics, but his song told of being married so many years that your wedding ring gets tarnished. It seemed to make him happy. We visited with him for a while and as we were leaving, he sang us out of the room. That was a first."

Sometimes the patients were feeling uneasy, frightened, and perhaps not in the mood for a visit, but Carol and Edith had developed ways to pique their interest. Edith might start by telling them about the hundreds of crafters and volunteers working in the community to create these items *just for them*. The patients frequently perked up and started asking questions, and in the process, became much more receptive. Carol would have usually opened the cart by this time and the patient might ask, "Do you have anything in blue? "Thank goodness, we were usually able to accommodate their requests, Edith said.

Carol shared a visit they had with a patient one afternoon. "We walked into the room of this young gal, whom I would estimate to be in her late teens. When we mentioned afghan, it was clear from her expression she was thinking 'old fashioned.' We knew right away that she would need something lively. Sure enough, when we looked at our trove of afghans, there was one in vibrant shades of red, blue, yellow, and green. We held it up for her and she said, 'I *love* that one.' She beamed and hugged it tightly. Then she started chatting with us about her journey related to her medical condition and her family. She had been in and out of hospitals, being treated for her cancer for years. Then her face lit with joy as she burst out laughing—'But I've *never* received a gift as a patient before.'"

Edith told of a patient they found sitting in the dark. They tapped lightly on her door and asked if she might like a visit. She shrugged and finally nodded. As they showed her the items on the cart, her curiosity was piqued. She turned the lights on and chose an afghan in vivid shades of pink and rose, as well as a neck roll pillow and bedside pocket pouch, both in pink. They could see this young patient visibly relax and she opened up to them. "When I was first brought to this room, I had received news that devastated me. I was feeling very sorry for myself and worried about my future. I was crying and didn't think I wanted to see *anyone.* But when you ladies came in being so quiet and respectful, offering me all these beautiful hand-made gifts, you lifted my spirits and made my day. I'm so glad you stopped by."

Carol and Edith learned that sometimes the patients just wanted to chat, to talk about the family they were missing, their children, grandchildren, dog, cat, parakeet. And while they were talking, they weren't thinking about their illness or their worries. Quite often, the spouse might have been through so much as their wife or husband had suffered and *they* needed to unload a bit. When it was clear they needed some comfort, these kind volunteers asked if they'd like a hug. Almost always the answer was a definite *yes*, as huge smiles spread across their faces!

*

Little Things?

A single sunbeam is enough to drive away many shadows.

– St. Francis of Assisi, Italian Catholic friar,
deacon, and preacher

Healing Ambassadors Marilyn and Barbara entered a patient's room one morning and asked how her day was going so far. Her response came quickly. "Awful! I didn't sleep at all last night. I woke up at 2:00 a.m., thought of several questions I should have asked my doctor yesterday, and didn't dare go back to sleep for fear of forgetting them. I had no paper, no pen, no cell phone."

Marilyn was so inspired by this patient's dilemma that she went home and sewed the prototype for what became known as "the bedside pocket pouch." She brought it in the next day and we all loved it. Designed to keep small items close at hand, we would also tuck a pad of paper and pencil inside. These pouches could be attached to either bedrail with a Velcro closure to keep small items organized and close by. The original rounded bottom was later altered to a rectangular shape to accommodate tablets.

Bedside Pocket Pouch

What might have been an insignificant inconvenience under normal circumstances took on major significance in the hospital setting. Edith and Carol witnessed a perfect example of this fact upon entering the room of a very agitated man who had been asked to sign some medical release forms. Understandably, he wanted to read them prior to signing. He had come to the hospital by ambulance under emergency conditions and had left his reading glasses behind on his bedside table at home. Fortunately, reading glasses were stocked on the cart and with these he was able to complete the process.

They came to the rescue of another patient who was similarly upset due to the lack of glasses, making it impossible for him to read the sports page to check on his teams. Now that's a real tragedy for a sports fan!

*

Challah and Comfort

Human greatness does not lie in wealth or power, but in character and goodness.

– Anne Frank, German-born Dutch-Jewish diarist and Holocaust victim

In May of 2008, Iris's granddaughter Ruby was born at Children's Hospital of Philadelphia (CHOP). Ruby never left the hospital and passed away in August. While at CHOP, this Jewish family received challah deliveries each Friday, brought by volunteers. Challah, the special bread eaten on the sabbath (Shabbat), which begins at sundown on Friday evenings, is one of the symbols used to welcome the sabbath. The two loaves of challah (a double portion for Friday and Saturday) are blessed, along with wine or grape juice as Jewish families gather and give thanks for these symbols of life-giving sustenance. Iris and her family were so grateful for these gifts from the hospital that helped them maintain some semblance of normalcy during their difficult time.

A month after Ruby's death, Iris was visiting her friend Fran, then a patient at St. Mary. As she walked into the room, Iris noticed a challah on Fran's tray, and asked where she had gotten it. Fran told her St. Mary had just started this challah delivery program. Iris knew immediately she wanted to participate. To honor Ruby's memory, Iris became a Shabbat challah deliverer and a No One Dies Alone volunteer.

In the ten years she had been a volunteer at St. Mary, she'd only cried once in a patient's room. It was a Friday, and she was on her challah rounds. She entered the room of a woman in her fifties who was near death. This woman's father was also a patient, but on a different floor. His nurses had brought him to his daughter's room to say goodbye. This father's farewell was so poignant, there wasn't a dry eye in the room. His nurses were crying, her nurses were crying, as well as the social worker and hospice caregiver. And as tears streamed down Iris's face, she hugged the grieving father. The solidarity of their response proved to be a beautiful means of "being with" this eighty-year-old man as his daughter left him. He wasn't alone; the room was full of people emoting and sharing his grief, human to human.

Iris was also asked to sit with a dementia patient one day. This visit was one of the most unusual she ever experienced. The patient, Genevieve, was easily in her nineties with beautiful long white hair. Iris introduced herself and Genevieve began an animated conversation. She told of her husband who was coming to get her soon and they were going to a wedding. It was evident that she was in her own world, so Iris joined her.

She asked Genevieve to tell her about the dress she would be wearing. She excitedly described a beautiful royal blue velvet gown with a detailed white lace collar. (Iris was able to vividly imagine how striking Genevieve would look in the gown with her lovely white hair flowing around her shoulders.)

In the next moment, Genevieve was gripping her back as if in great pain and said she was in labor. Iris was startled by the dramatic shift in subject and mood, but coached her through her labor, encouraging her to breathe and pant. She stayed with Genevieve until her eyelids became heavy and she said, "I'm really tired now and ready to go to sleep, so you can leave." She peacefully relaxed, and Iris stepped out, quite exhausted herself.

When she got to her car, she called her daughter Amy who is a social worker at a nursing home. She works with dementia patients on a regular basis. Iris asked her if she had done the right thing. Amy replied, "Mommy, you went into her world, and how comforting for that person."

When Iris arrived for her challah deliveries, she always checked the list of patients to be visited that day. Through her previous work in the Jewish community for many years, she had come to know many people. If any of the names were familiar, she arranged her visits so that they were last, which enabled her to have a longer visit with them, and possibly family members as well.

One of her visits was with a young man who had been in her daughter's social work class. Unfortunately, he suffered with a very serious gastric disorder. When a patient is unable to take anything orally, a sign with the letters NPO (*nil per os*—nothing by mouth) is posted on their door. As Iris entered, she knew he wouldn't be able to enjoy any of the delicious challah. She made him promise not to sneak any.

"I'll leave this for your parents, siblings, and your girlfriend." In these cases, though she knew the patient would be unable to eat the challah, she still felt it was important for them to receive this symbol of welcoming the sabbath.

With heartfelt emotion, Iris concluded, "I was so grateful the challah program existed at St. Mary and at CHOP to enable the patients confined in these hospitals, to still take part in this important aspect of the Jewish tradition. Bread is life. Bread is love. And I was grateful to be able to make these deliveries to honor the memory of my precious grandchild, Ruby."

*

Respite Companions

Volunteers are paid in six figures…S-M-I-L-E-S.

– Gayla Lemaire, American

By 2009, the Healing Environments Program included Healing Ambassadors and the NODA Comfort Companions who kept vigil at the bedside of dying patients. (Refer to Chapter Ten for more details). However, we soon became aware of the potential for another position between these two. We would sometimes receive calls from the nurses who described a patient in need of special attention, people who might be feeling worried and anxious about up-coming surgery or treatment, or someone who, for whatever reason, couldn't be soothed. Due to the nurses' other patients and duties, they weren't able to be with these patients for extended periods of time.

Respite Companions were the answer. These volunteers were able to stay with the patients, listen to them, read to them, play cards, and discuss sports or other interests. By visiting with the patients, the Respite Companions helped to take the patients' minds off their troubles, passing the time more pleasantly, and helping them remain calm. And without question this new aspect of the Healing Environments Program became one of the nurses' absolute favorites.

*

Sharing Their Faith

*Help one another; there's no time like the present
and no present like the time.*

– James Durst, American author

While conducting his work as a Respite Companion one day, Nino had a particularly memorable experience. When he arrived on the oncology unit, he checked in at the nurses' station to ask if there were any patients who might especially benefit from a visit. The unit clerk directed him to the room of a patient who had just returned from an oncology treatment and was feeling depressed.

He went to her door, tapped lightly, and greeted the patient. In heavily accented English she said, "You're not Jewish, so why are you here?"

Nino replied, "No, I'm not Jewish, but I'm here for you, to visit and bring you comfort. I'd be happy to recite the Mi Sheberach prayer for you." (This is the Hebrew prayer asking God to heal the sick.) The translation follows:

May the Source of Strength who blessed the ones
*   before us,*
Help us find the courage to make our lives a blessing.
And let us say, Amen
Bless those in need of healing with refuah sh'leimah
The renewal of body, the renewal of spirit.
And let us say, Amen

Nino then started to say the three-fold Priestly Blessing and she joined in:

May the Lord bless you and keep you.
May the Lord make His face shed light upon you and
*   be gracious to you.*
May the Lord lift His face unto you and give you peace.
"You know my religion!" she exclaimed.
"Yes, I do," he said, "it's the same as mine. My Christian faith has its basis in Judaism."
She tearfully told him that he had made her day.

As mentioned in Chapter Two, inclusivity was always of primary importance at St Mary. Not only were various religions represented within the patient population, among the staff, and volunteers, but employees and volunteers who spoke other languages were also sought to aid patients struggling with a foreign language while also dealing with their medical issues.

*

A Compassionate Presence

One of the sincerest forms of respect is actually listening to what another has to say.

– Herbert H. McGill, American author

In 2002, Bob's mother notified him that his dad had been taken to the hospital with what seemed to be pneumonia. Following further tests and diagnoses, his diagnosis was deemed to be mesothelioma. After working in environments containing asbestos most of his life, it had taken its toll. His father was given three months to live; he died three weeks later. His father's hospice caregiver made a significant impression on their family. Bob watched her as she gently cared for his dad and also appreciated how she showed such compassion to the whole family. With Bob and his family gathered at the bedside, his dad passed peacefully to God.

This painful and deeply meaningful experience was the catalyst for Bob to become a volunteer, to give back. He had been searching for that opportunity when he learned about the volunteer program at St. Mary.

"I met Joan, and she made such a significant first impression on me. After extensive training and orientation, I felt privileged to become a Respite Companion."

As part of this program, he had many opportunities to work with patients all over the hospital, visiting with them and their families, listening, and being a compassionate presence. Bob enjoyed making use of the gifts provided on the Healing Cart. He offered the patients and family members items such as crossword puzzles, word finders, newspapers, handmade shawls, afghans, neck roll pillows, rosaries, and prayer books to enhance their time in the hospital and help their days pass more pleasantly.

One day he was called to the room of a man who had been pressing the nurses' call button all morning. The patient was facing surgery the following day and was visibly agitated. The nurses informed Bob of the patient's state of mind and also told him the patient was an avid Phillies fan. They asked him to be sure to bring the sports page. As a loyal Phillies fan himself, Bob was looking forward to chatting about his favorite team. "I grabbed the paper and my Phillies ball cap before heading to his room. When I walked in wearing my cap, his face lit up and we shared an immediate rapport. We talked baseball, sports in general, I read him some articles, and we thoroughly enjoyed more than two hours together. He reminisced about taking his children and grandchildren to the games, how it always made his day to see them all cheer for the 'home team.' I guess I wore him out because his eyes began to close, but I left him with a happy smile on his face."

*

The Veteran Appreciation Program

The soldier above all others prays for peace, for it is the soldier who must suffer and bear the deepest wounds and scars of war.

– Douglas MacArthur, American five-star general and field marshal of the Philippine Army

In 2015, the volunteers and crafters were asked to take part in a new initiative to thank our in-patients who were veterans or active-duty military personnel. Two nurses, whose sons were serving in Iraq at the time, felt strongly that St. Mary should honor all of our veterans. The Healing Environments volunteers began cutting and tying blankets made from fleece imprinted with American flags, stars, and red, white, and blue designs. I also asked those already making neck roll pillows if they would sew some using the same fleece. They enthusiastically agreed.

We enlisted the help of three volunteers already working in various positions who were veterans themselves, Bob, Jim, and Rita, to deliver the blankets and pillows to any veteran in the hospital. Quite often, these deliveries led to more than our opportunity to personally thank these people who had defended our nation and became a meaningful visit with a fellow vet.

From its inception in March 2015 until March 2017, over 1,500 veterans were visited and presented with their veteran appreciation gifts. The program is still on-going.

VOLUNTEER SERVICES

(Left to Right) Robert Crisci,St. Mary Veteran Volunteer; Joan Portman, Coordinator of the Healing Environments Veteran Appreciation Program; James Frawley, St. Mary Veteran Volunteer; Terri Rivera, St. Mary Vice President for Mission and Community Health; and Rita Wagner, St. Mary Veteran Volunteer.

Healing Environments Veteran Appreciation Program Getting Big Boost Thanks to St. Mary Medical Center's 6th Annual Cupcake Wars

On Thursday, November 10, Terri Rivera, St. Mary Medical Center's Vice President for Mission and Community Health, presented a check for **$2,400** to Joan Portman, coordinator of the hospital's Healing Environments Veteran Appreciation Program. The funds came directly from the proceeds of the hospital's 6th Annual Cupcake Wars.

The Veteran Appreciation Program offers veteran patients the choice of either a hand tied fleece blanket, crochet military blanket or neck roll pillow. Each veteran also receives a St Mary Appreciation Wristband, which encourages other colleagues to thank our veterans for their service.

"St. Mary recognizes the great sacrifices our veterans have made for us so we can live in a free and just society," says Portman. "They have given so much for us in service to this country. This is our way of thanking them for that service."

The money raised will enable the Veteran Appreciation Program volunteers to purchase the military patterned fleece they use to hand-sew the blankets and neck rolls.

Vet Fleece and Reprint of Newsletter Articles

Jim, a Vietnam vet, and active volunteer at St. Mary, enjoyed this program very much. His great smile and big voice had a way of putting people at ease and helping them know he was safe to talk to. He welcomed this special opportunity to be a spokesman for St. Mary to express their heartfelt appreciation to those who had sacrificed for their country. "I know every veteran I greet gave of themselves to help keep our country safe and strong. That knowledge humbles me. I also have an immediate rapport with Vietnam vets who got the worst deal. We were humiliated and deprived of the honor and respect normally afforded returning soldiers. It gives me a special sense of accomplishment to be able to visit with these guys and finally express our gratitude to them."

*

Honoring Our Veterans

It is a proud privilege to be a soldier – a good soldier with discipline, self-respect, pride in his unit and his country.

– George S. Patton, Jr., General, United States Army, WWII

Naval veteran Bob C thoroughly enjoyed visiting veterans at St. Mary. Although his opening "lines" were usually the same, introducing himself as a naval vet, and informing the patient of his purpose to express the hospital's appreciation for the patient's service, he received many unique responses.

Bob told us of some of his visits. "Some guys said, 'Thanks. Nice blanket.' And that was it. Others might get into a conversation, while others couldn't speak, but their spouse or family member enthusiastically expressed their gratitude. This occurred especially in the ICU and CCU where the patients' physical condition might prevent them from speaking. Often the relatives got very excited and sometimes emotional as their loved one was receiving acknowledgement and being honored in this way."

He found that frequently these blankets almost took on the significance of the American flag for some recipients. One vet Bob visited was deeply touched.

"This big guy, a Vietnam vet, was lying in the bed. As I told him I was there to express our appreciation and present him with this blanket, he broke down sobbing. As he clutched the blanket tightly in his arms, he eventually calmed enough to say, 'Nobody ever gave me anything for serving over there or ever thanked me.' Considering how poorly we received our returning Vietnam soldiers, if this program can help heal some of *those* deep wounds, it will definitely be a success."

If the patient was a navy vet, he and Bob might have a fifteen- to twenty-minute visit. If a former marine was lying in the bed, that was an opportunity for teasing. Bob might remark, "Oh, Semper Fi, don't worry, I won't hold it against you." They'd chuckle good naturedly and perhaps shoot the breeze for a few minutes. In almost all cases, Bob left the veterans in a better state of mind.

A small number of the veterans were women. One such patient's baby had been born prematurely and therefore needed to be in an incubator on the Neonatal Intensive Care Unit. Bob asked the nurses if he would be able to visit the new mom and present her blanket. They all agreed his visit would be wonderful to help lift her spirits. As she received her gift, she gave Bob a huge smile and thanked him for helping her through a tough time.

Bob usually visited between fifteen to twenty-five veterans a day. "The most blankets I ever gave out was thirty-four. Even without a lot of chatter, it took several hours. The patients were spread out in almost every unit in the hospital."

Most of these patients had served in World War II, the Korean Conflict, Vietnam, or the Gulf War. But sometimes the guys didn't feel they deserved the blanket because they hadn't served during wartime. Bob always assured them if they had signed up and served, wartime or not, they were still vets and were definitely entitled to receive a blanket and St. Mary's gratitude.

*

Healing War Wounds

Thank you for the cost you paid for our freedom, thank you for the freedom to live in safety and pursue happiness.

– Sara Niles, daughter of marine staff sergeant Erik Niles
and Laurie Niles, to the Veterans of the
United States of America

Jim's military experience provides him an immediate connection with the veterans, especially the Vietnam vets. "I came back with Agent Orange, but when I walk into a vet's room, introduce myself, state my purpose to express appreciation for their service on behalf of the hospital, they welcome me. When I tell them I was in Nam and came back with Agent Orange, I often see tears glimmering in their eyes and some openly weep, especially those suffering similar illnesses. We have this unfortunate alliance, but it helps them open up and release some anger, pain, and frustration. Many confide that they've held the bitterness bottled up inside since the war. They find it a great relief to be able to talk openly about their feelings and let go."

Jim shared, "Others who were in the service during the war, but who weren't sent to Nam, are still carrying around guilt about it. I advise them to drop the guilt, telling them they would have gone if they'd been assigned. I still warmly thank them and give them their blanket. Sometimes the vet is out of the room for surgery or a treatment, but their wife or family members are there. They *love* receiving the blanket and are always amazed that the hospital cares enough to reach out in this unique and unexpected way."

"I visited with a British soldier who shared some interesting military experiences from the Brit's point of view. We spoke for quite a while, but as he started to tire, I asked if he'd like one of the blankets. 'Sure, mate,' he said, with a huge smile and a vigorous handshake."

*

Football, WWII, and Prayers

One of the interesting things about volunteering is that while you are there to give, you also receive a tremendous amount in return.

– Bob P., American volunteer

During a recent Respite Companion visit at St. Mary, Bob stopped by the nurses' station to ask if there was anyone who needed special attention. The nurse guided him to Ed's room, saying some of his family members were there and might need assistance. The patient's daughter, Susan, and a friend were sitting next to her father Ed. After introducing himself, he asked if there was anything they needed. Ed's daughter gratefully said yes that she really needed coffee! He was happy to oblige and brought her some. While her father slept, Bob chatted with the visitors for a while. Susan asked if Bob might be available the following night to visit with her dad after dinner and stay at his bedside until he fell asleep. The family would not be able to be there in the evening and would be sincerely grateful if someone could stay with him. Bob readily agreed to keep Ed company and help in any way he could.

Bob arrived Saturday evening and was told by the nurse that he had just missed the family, but that Ed was awake in his room, eating and watching the Notre Dame/Navy football game. They hit it off right away thanks to their common interest in college football! To Bob's surprise, Ed was quite chatty and had a lot to say on various topics: football, his military service, including World War II, and his family. He had served in the army and had fought at the Battle of the Bulge. He was wrapped in one of the Veteran Appreciation blankets and enjoying its warmth. What an interesting guy!

Ed's hand was a bit unsteady, so Bob helped him to finish his drink from dinner. They spent some enjoyable time together while Ed relaxed. Just before seven p.m., the nurses came in to change his bedding. Bob stepped out and when he came back about ten minutes later, Ed had fallen asleep. Bob recited a prayer for him, said good night, and told him he'd see him the next day.

After church Bob arrived at St. Mary hoping to visit Ed and his family. As he approached Ed's room, he noticed the door was closed with a sign posted to "See the nurse." The unit clerk informed him that the patient had passed away shortly before five a.m. that morning. Bob was stunned by this news, considering what a lively and interesting conversation they had enjoyed the previous night. His feelings were clear on his face, and the nurse gave him a comforting hug. The dichotomy of this situation was that Bob was coming to the hospital intending to bring comfort to Ed and his family, and instead he was receiving comfort from one of the wonderful staff. When Bob saw Ed's obituary in the paper several weeks later, he went to the viewing. There, he had the pleasure of meeting many members of Ed's family and learned more about this World War II veteran. But what stood out most powerfully about this man was the importance of family in his life.

8

More Ways to Make a Difference

Pet Therapy

I have found when you are deeply troubled, there are things you get from the silent devoted companionship of a dog that you can get from no other source.

– Doris Day, American actress, singer, and animal welfare activist

In this chapter, we delve into the wide diversity of volunteer opportunities, which were also included under the Healing Environments "umbrella." Stories from pet therapists, musicians, as well as programs specifically designed for cardiac patients are featured.

(Resource information about these groups can be found in Chapter Thirteen, Taking Action.)

*

Personality Plus

If there are no dogs in Heaven, then when I die,
I want to go where they went.

– Will Rogers, American stage and film actor,
vaudeville performer, cowboy, and humorist

Lynne and her beloved basset hound Oberon visited the hospital not only for the patients, their families, and visitors, but also for the staff, whose work is so hard. Some of Obie's favorite staff friends would see him from the other end of the hall and shout, "Hey O!" and come running to give him a pat, a hug, or a treat. He even knew where some of their offices were and went directly to their doors and moaned to be let in for his treats.

During one of their hospital visits, they had an interesting conversation with Janet, one of the oncology patients. Lynne always put some special outfit on Obie for the holidays to bring some cheer and chuckles for the patients and staff. On that day, he had a Statue of Liberty hat on. They entered Janet's room and greeted her warmly. During previous visits, Janet hadn't usually responded. On this day she said, "He hates the hat." That brought smiles all around.

They were visiting the infusion room one day when a patient they had been visiting regularly for weeks was petting Oberon. She leaned toward Lynne and in a whisper confided, "I really don't like dogs, but I like *him!* He has such personality."

Quite often they stopped at rooms where a loved one sat nervously waiting while the patient was in another part of the hospital undergoing a test or procedure. As Lynne and Obie walked in, they often saw the person's eyes light up, faces relax a bit as they experienced the calming influence dogs can have on people. She and Obie also visited the Same Day Surgery waiting room, where they offered a much-needed diversion for those anxiously awaiting news of their loved one's condition.

Lynne told about a very interesting experience the two had with an Alzheimer's patient. When they first tried to visit with her, she pretended to be sleeping. Gradually, as days passed, she would move her hand to the edge of the bed to touch Obie (still pretending to be sleeping). Eventually, she actually looked forward to his visits. Obie won her over.

This dynamic duo also visited a school for autistic children to offer emotional support. One day a little boy was having a particularly hard time. Joshua was spread out on his sleep mat and Oberon stretched out beside him. Soon Obie fell asleep and began to snore loudly. Joshua said, "Dog, wake up, I'm reading to you." And indeed, he pretended to read to Obie from the storybook he was holding.

A little girl newly arrived from Denmark, fell in love with Oberon immediately. Isabel was in second grade and just learning English. Her teacher very wisely used Oberon to create a game to help this young girl learn the parts of the body. The teacher would ask, "Where is Obie's nose? And where is your nose?" The little girl would point to Obie's and then to her own, while Oberon sat patiently. She learned very quickly, thanks to Obie and Lynne's visits, and the learning was fun.

Oberon especially loved to visit the infusion room at St. Mary. Patients received chemotherapy or transfusions in this area and might be there for four to five hours. Obie made many friends with the patients who were there week after week. One patient who was receiving infusions over a period of months looked forward to Obie's visits so much that when Lynne had to change their day to visit, the patient changed her infusion day so that she could still see Obie. And he especially loved visits to this area because the staff gave him his favorite treats.

Lynne confided her gratitude for being able to do this work. "Visiting these patients was very humbling and also made me appreciate my own health. I've been doing this work for more than thirty years, and I pray I'll be able to continue for many more."

*

Needing Winston

Dogs are not our whole life, but they make our lives whole.

– Roger A. Caras, American wildlife photographer, writer,
wildlife preservationist, and TV personality

"I need a visit with Winston." This beautiful English springer spaniel and owner Karen were very popular among the patients and received frequent patient requests. Karen began her forty-year career as a nurse and nursing educator in the operating room as a surgical RN. Now retired, she and pal Winston regularly visited the patients at St. Mary. Winston, who was definitely a "people dog," might have several patients follow him down the hall to be able to prolong their visit.

As Karen said, "It's like being able to talk to your neighbors over the fence…just in a hospital setting. It brings a sense of normalcy to the lives of the patients and their families. Patients, especially those who are very ill, and their families need and want a diversion in their day, distraction form their pain and anxiety. They may be missing their own pet(s). I frequently noticed our visits acted as an 'icebreaker' to help the patients open up."

One day as they walked down the hall during a visit, family members of a patient were standing outside the room. As Karen and Winston approached, the patient's daughter, Marie, spoke as she knelt to pet Winston and looked up at Karen with tears coursing down her cheeks. "Thank you so much for being here today. Our mother is dying, but we've always had dogs and she loved them. It means so much to have you come. She's very close to death, but we'll tell her you're both here to be with her."

They all walked back into the room and as Marie told her mother about her visitors, Winston put his paws up on the bed so that her hand could touch his silky fur. She lay still with her eyes closed, but a slight smile fleetingly touched her lips. She died very peacefully shortly after their visit.

*

Music Therapy– The Universal Language

Music is the language of the Spirit. It opens the secret of life-bringing peace, abolishing strife.

– Kahlil Gibran, Lebanese American writer, poet, and visual artist

We found that music was an ideal means of calming our patients. But as you read in Chapter Five, "Rockin' to Heaven", it is also very personal. We therefore had a large library of CDs. However, when Angelo played his harp in the corridors, staff, patients, and visitors stilled to listen.

*

Angelo's Harp

Sing unto the Lord with the harp, with the harp, and the voice of a psalm.

Psalm 98:5

Soft harp music drifted through the corridor as I stepped onto the oncology unit. Two weeks before Christmas, Chaplain Angelo DeLorenzo had come to play holiday favorites for the patients who unfortunately had to be in the hospital at this time. Their families and most certainly the staff loved to hear Angelo play "O Tannenbaum," "The Hallelujah Chorus," and "O Holy Night," to name a few. Sometimes children, visiting a family member, would come running out of rooms to stand close and watch him play, fascinated as his fingers strummed and plucked the strings. Other visitors would come to stand at the open doorways of the patients' rooms to drink in the sometimes soothing, sometimes joyful melodies. The staff always loved Angelo's time spent on their units, a special gift to them as well. His music lightened the moods of many and brought smiles of appreciation.

"Playing the harp is one of the most joyful and important parts of my ministry throughout the year, Angelo confided. I have about two hours of music I can play, including showtunes, classical, operatic, and popular selections. It's a beautiful sight to see Alzheimer's and dementia patients tapping their toes or fingers to the beat of tunes they still recognize.

"One day I was playing on the cardiac unit. Aides constantly monitor the patients' heart rates and blood pressures, as well as other levels. After commenting that the harp music was so soothing and relaxing, one of the aides offered to keep a record of her two patients' levels specifically during the time I was playing. Both patients' heart rates and blood pressures went down during that time with no other changes in stimuli."

*

Touching an Inner Chord

Music speaks what cannot be expressed, soothes the mind, and gives it rest, heals the heart, and makes it whole, flows from Heaven to the soul.

– Author Unknown

Candi is our organist and also plays the piano in the lobby of the hospital. Candi is also blind, but her deep love of music and delight in sharing it with others inspires and invigorates her.

She plays the piano each Tuesday morning and her organ music is piped from the chapel to the hospital rooms in the afternoon. During the weeks prior to Christmas, she played her extensive holiday repertoire. Many people stopped to express their appreciation for her joyful contribution, which created a welcoming atmosphere at the hospital entrance.

One woman told her she had come to spend time with her mother, who was upstairs close to death. This daughter was understandably distraught about her mother's condition. As she came back down and exited the elevator, Candi's music greeted her. Instead of leaving, the woman decided to sit in the lobby and listen to Candi play. As Candi finished one song, this lady took the opportunity to come to the piano, and briefly described how she had been feeling and how Candi's music had lifted a tremendous weight from her shoulders. She confided to Candi, "I feel you were sent by my mother, also a great lover of music, to ease my grief. Your music deeply touched my heart."

*

Heart Therapy

There is no better exercise for your heart than reaching down and helping someone up.

– Bernard Meltzer, American radio personality

*

Zipper Club

The Zipper Club was already in existence in 2008. Volunteers who had undergone open heart surgery themselves visited patients who had recently undergone the procedure. The fact that these volunteers were up and out, living their lives and carrying on with important work gave the patients and their families hope that they too could recover and move forward with their own lives.

These volunteers visited the patients with a special zest, having been given a second chance at life. They were tremendously kind and took special care with fellow heart patients to help them understand feelings and situations that might arise post-surgically. These volunteers provided a vital connecting thread to help the patients look toward a useful and positive future.

*

WOMENHEART

WOMENHEART was the first national patient-centered organization dedicated to serving women with heart disease [Appendix III]. The program was introduced at St. Mary to help educate and empower women living with or at risk of heart disease. The little-known fact is that while some symptoms of heart disease in women can be the same as those for men (shortness of breath, chest pain, tightness or pressure, dizziness, or nausea), other symptoms such as back or shoulder pain or heartburn can also occur in women. These symptoms can unfortunately be attributed to other health issues. Because of this fact, women can have a heart attack, collapse, be brought to the emergency department, and wake up in the hospital not having a *clue* why they're here.

WOMENHEART Ambassadors visit these patients in the cardiac unit to help them become accustomed to their situation. These volunteers could develop an immediate rapport with the patients since they were also living with cardiac issues themselves.

The crafters were asked to crochet or knit red scarves to be given out during the fall and winter months, and heart-shaped keychains needlepointed with red yarn* during the other times of year. Of course, the answer was, "Yes, we'll make those too."

The WOMENHEART Ambassadors found that these gifts, along with the information packets offered to the patients, helped to eliminate a bit of the stress and fear being experienced by these newly diagnosed heart patients.

*Red Heart Yarn Company generously donated the yarn for these projects.

9

Bringing Spiritual Comfort

I've learned that people will forget what you said, people will forget what you did, but people will never forget how you made them feel.

– Maya Angelou, American poet, singer, memoirist, and civil rights activist

The Spiritual Care Department staff provided the following stories.

St. Mary is a Catholic hospital originally founded by Sisters of St. Francis. However, many faiths are represented among the staff and in the patient population. The inclusivity I mentioned in the first chapter as I walked the corridors and saw illustrated in the photos of so many religious sites around the globe, was practiced every day. The spiritual caregivers endeavored to make sure the patients felt accepted and at ease no matter what their religious preference, race, or nationality.

*

A Priest's Gift of Serenity

Yea, though I walk through the valley of the
shadow of death, I will fear no evil,
for You are with me.

– Psalm 23:4

Ed, the patriarch of his family and an observant Jew, lay near death. He was covered with the handmade afghan the volunteers had brought in burgundy, navy, and charcoal grey. His distraught wife and family members had gathered to keep their vigil. Their rabbi unfortunately wouldn't be able to get to the hospital until later that day.

I had become friendly with Ed's daughter and could see she was extremely anxious. I quietly asked if she would like me to have one of the chaplains or priests come. She tearfully replied, "Oh, yes please."

Father Raju arrived within minutes from the spiritual care department, bringing his loving presence. I had previously experienced an aura of tranquility that filled the space whenever he walked into a patient's room. It was as if the family had been holding its collective breath, and at last could exhale and release some of the tension. In his rich melodious Indian accent,

Father Raju introduced himself to each member of the family. He gently placed his hand on Ed's wife's shoulder as he softly murmured psalms at the bedside. And when Ed passed, he recited blessings for him in Hebrew. As he blessed her dad, he shared tears with the family who were so grateful to receive his sincere expressions of sympathy. Years later as I spoke with Ed's daughter, she mentioned her deep gratitude that Father Raju had honored her father by reciting Hebrew blessings he knew would bring this devout Jewish family the most comfort.

Several years later, her mother was also stricken with cancer, and again the volunteers visited, bringing a beautiful afghan, and again Father Raju was there to console the family. In a heartfelt letter to the CEO, she wrote, "This type of caring and love from people we didn't even know had a tremendous effect on emotions beyond describing."

Then, in 2013, she was diagnosed with cancer, and was at St. Mary for surgery. I visited with her the day after her procedure. When I offered her an afghan and an anti-ouch pouch, she tried to decline, but I insisted, knowing these gifts are not just about the items themselves. They also bring the blessings and prayers stitched into every item, as well as the concept that others "out there" are thinking of the patient and care about them and their welfare.

In her letter she wrote, "Not everyone can understand the importance of these gestures unless they experience cancer. It is very isolating, whether you have a supportive family or have no one. There is a bond that forms with someone you don't know who shares and cares for you. It helps! It is enough to keep you going through tough times."

*

Spiritual Encounters

People are not problems to be solved.
They are mysteries to be explored.

– Eugene Peterson, American Presbyterian minister,
scholar, theologian, author, and poet

Jack Geracci, Director of Spiritual Care Services, shared the following experience. "One of our colleagues recently passed away at the hospital. While waiting for the bus, she suffered a cardiac arrest, was immediately given CPR, then taken to the emergency department. But she died shortly thereafter, despite all efforts to revive her. She was originally from Cuba, and we didn't have good contact information for her next of kin. We were eventually able to get in touch with her niece who lives in the area and her sister from Florida."

When they arrived, Jack escorted them to view her body. The viewing room in the morgue is, of necessity, a cold and sterile environment. So, Jack thought to bring one of the Healing Environments afghans with which to cover the patient. Though no one could deny the physical chill of the room, the beautiful soft blanket made such a difference for the family. The blanket was given to her sister to crystallize this moment and give her something tangible in memory of her sister.

Though Jack had been in healthcare for forty years, an RN at another location, this was the first time the thought occurred to him to offer the family this form of comfort. He witnessed firsthand the distinct positive effect it had on the colleague's family, as it helped them to feel welcomed after traveling so far, and it simultaneously expressed our respect for their loved one.

Jack also directs the Certified Educator of the chaplain interns at the hospital. Often, these young people came directly from college campuses and seminaries to the very strange, uncomfortable, and unfamiliar hospital setting. When they first arrived, they were understandably ill at ease and at a loss as to how to approach patients at the bedside. After establishing relationships with patients, and providing spiritual care, the students were able to extend their ministry by presenting Healing Environments items such as afghans, neck roll pillows, and blessing cards. Some patients felt more comfortable with any one of these items. And the ability to offer these gifts helped the interns create a bridge with the patients and expanded the pastoral encounter.

With the cheerful addition of these vibrant hand-made items, a clear message of caring was sent to the patients and their families. And the time given by the volunteers who delivered them helped the patients' days pass more comfortably and with less stress. Reading materials, crossword, word find, and sudoku books were also appreciated. In an effort to go beyond providing excellent clinical patient care, the establish-ment of the Healing Environments Program enabled us to tangibly express our desire to treat the patients' body, mind, and spirit.

The chaplains and interns appreciate the blanket blessing card wrapped with each gift. It enables them to open the door to spiritual conversations with the patients, some of whom are angry with life, with God, and with their situation. In addition, through music therapy, pet therapy, other gifts of comfort and conve-nience, we were able to bring tangible enhancements to the unsettling hospital surroundings, making them more home-like.

As he walked past the Healing Gardens on a lovely sunny day, Jack saw that one of the nurses had brought a young oncology patient outside for some much-needed fresh air. The young woman had been a patient at St. Mary for quite a while. It inspired him to see that the nurse, as busy as nurses are, was taking the time to treat this patient to a taste of nature and a bit of normalcy, which brought refreshing comfort to her entire being.

Jack strongly believes that providing the best possible care for people often experiencing desperate situations requires thinking creatively, sometimes "outside the box," going above and beyond and considering what services *we* would want to receive if we were in the patients' position. "That is our ultimate intention."

*

Bringing God's Loving Presence

The memory of the righteous is a blessing.

– Proverbs 10:7

As a chaplain at St. Mary Medical Center for twenty years, Madeline Marr had the privilege of being in many patients' rooms in their final hours. These patients were losing everything; they had lost their health, those close to death were losing their lives, some were estranged from their families or had no community to call upon in their final days.

The afghans and comfort items provided by the Healing Environments Program enabled her to offer these patients something of value that they were able to receive. Time and again they were amazed that an ordinary person, a crafter, working from home creating this beautiful object would then choose to give it away to someone they didn't even know.

Madeline often considered herself a "Good Will Ambassador" as well as a chaplain. She knew that not everyone was interested in a visit from a spiritual representative, or a visit of any kind! As she entered a patient's room with the blanket in her arms, beautifully wrapped and ready for presentation, it enabled her to "get her foot in the door" so to speak. They may not initially have wanted someone to pray or be with them, but when she came "bearing gifts" and started talking about the beautiful afghans made by the crafters, they became interested.

She was then able to create a bond with the patients and their families. As she unwrapped the afghan from its plastic bag, removed the beautiful ribbon and spread the blanket over them, then read the blessing card, almost magically, a gateway would open to conversation. If the patient was alone, sometimes it became evident that they were lonely and down. In that case, Madeline became a loving presence and an active listener. At other times, perhaps the patient was sleeping or unconscious due to medication. Then she was able to speak with any family members present.

In all of these circumstances, the afghan was the "key" to opening the conversation. Madeline wanted them to know she was there for them, to be a kind, supportive, listening presence. Yes, she was also representing God, and whatever they thought God to be was certainly a factor, but the beautiful spiritual component was a palpable presence. She was received and enabled to conduct her ministry, as the lines of communication were opened. One seemingly "little thing" is that this afghan, shawl, or quilt created a sacred space, a safe haven where they were able to express emotions, fears, worries, or anxieties. They could cry freely, speak of their loved ones or estrangements, anger, deep and abiding love. And while in their presence, she prayed that whatever their spirit needed would be provided.

The patients she visited were sometimes experiencing deep sadness. She would hear such pain-filled comments as these:

"I haven't seen my dad in years. He left us and Mom when we were little."

"Our son was on drugs and caused us so much pain and heartache, but we still love him."

The handmade afghans, offered with Madeline's gentle approach, opened windows of opportunity for forgiveness and created a mantle of peace.

There were days when she was tired, when it was an effort for her to go to the volunteer office on the ground floor, get the afghans, then go all the way up to the fourth floor to the patients' rooms. But Madeline knew the power of these gifts and the positive impact they created, and not knowing if the patient would survive the night or be transferred the next day, the effort was worth it. Many times, as the patients and/or family members "oohed and aahed" over the blanket, her spirits were uplifted as well.

For the families of those who passed, these afghans took on an even more profound importance. They spoke on many occasions of how precious the blanket would be for them and their families, as the last thing to have touched their loved one. The patient's essence could be felt through the contact with their afghan. Sometimes they expressed their amazement at the color. "That was Mom's favorite color…how could you possibly have known?"

Madeline also *loved* to watch as new family members or friends arrived, and those keeping the bedside vigil would exclaim, "Look at this afghan they gave Dad! And it's a gift!"

It was obvious to these families that St. Mary cared enough to provide these special items, as well as state-of-the-art medical care and exceptional medical staff. She experienced time and again the ability of these blankets to create a space of healing, not necessarily in the medical meaning of that word, but in a deeper spiritual context. She may have entered a room where the patient was sad, withdrawn, lacking hope, and perhaps believing that no one cared. But that was not the person she left as she walked out their door. They knew without doubt that people indeed did care, and what a beautiful feeling that is.

*

Welcome to Heaven

Love and kindness are never wasted. They always make a difference. They bless the one who receives them, and they bless the giver.

– Barbara De Angeles, American relationship consultant, lecturer, and author

One of the most difficult and traumatic happenings in the hospital occurred when a patient died unexpectedly, when the family was not able to get to the hospital right away. The patient's body had to be moved to the morgue. Although every effort was made to make the viewing room hospitable, it was not the optimal place to see your loved one for the last time.

Chaplain Susie Minno was faced with this situation one night. A young man, Jim, had been seriously injured riding his motorcycle, was rushed to the hospital, but succumbed to his injuries. His family was notified, but it would be two hours before they could arrive. Susie fully understood the anguish they would be feeling and went into action to provide what comfort she could. She dashed to the volunteer office to get an afghan. Jim was tall, so she searched for and found a large one in shades of blue and burgundy.

She dashed back to the viewing room, unwrapped, and spread the blanket over his still form, set the blessing card nearby, dimmed the overhead lights, and lit the battery votive candles, which she placed around the room. She selected peaceful music, which played softly.

When Jim's parents and sister arrived, Susie was there to greet and console them and sat with them as they wept. When they were calmer, she read the blessing card and told them a little about the afghan, the crafters, and the Healing Environments Program. She assured them the blanket was theirs to keep in memory of their son and brother. She invited them to talk about Jim. She learned he was a hard-working student studying psychology with the hope of ultimately working with prisoners. He had a part-time job to help pay for school and drove the motorcycle to save money.

As sad as this experience was, the family was so grateful to Susie for her efforts to care for their son with such respect. She later received a thank you card from his parents in which they told her the blanket had covered his casket at the funeral. It was then taken to their home and placed in their den where they could see it every day and remember their son.

*

Each Moment of This Day

Every morning is a fresh beginning. Every day is the world made new. Today is a new day... This is my day of opportunity.

– Norman Vincent Peale - American Protestant clergyman, author, and speaker

I had the pleasure of interviewing Chaplain Shari who is also one of our crafters. I asked how she feels while making afghans and hair-loss caps for our patients, and does she weave prayers and blessings into these items?

"Absolutely, and especially because I have a two hour commute each way to and from St. Mary. Knitting and crocheting items that I know are of benefit to our patients helps me to feel purposeful while keeping me calm during the commute. The rhythm is healing and helps me to make the transition from the workday to my home life. While I'm making these items, others notice and it gives me the opportunity to tell them about the Healing Environments Program, and to share the values and mission of the hospital."

Shari also enjoys using the small yarn balls inevitably left over after larger projects have been completed. She purposely looks in the craft cabinets for these small quantities (some no larger than a golf ball) to use together with others to create full-size colorful afghans. Nothing goes to waste! The happy results of Shari's efforts are not only beautiful one-of-a-kind afghans, but also saving these small yarn balls from going to a landfill. "It challenges me creatively to work with so many colors while making sure the results are a symphony and not a cacophony."

She also appreciates the fact that St. Mary provides lovely acrylic yarn to be used by the crafters. It retains its softness and is easy care (machine wash and dry), which is especially important for patients who are not feeling well. Some of the blankets are stored on the ICU where Shari works. The stock needs to be replenished frequently, as the nurses love the opportunity to give them out. The blankets provide the nursing staff with something tangible for the patient to hold on to in times of trouble and stress.

Intensive Care Units are places of waiting, waiting for a test, waiting for results. Shari often notices the family members holding the patient's blanket while they wait anxiously for their loved one to return from a test or procedure. ICUs are also necessarily sterile and serious environments with all the intimidating equipment, so she enjoys being able to add a spot of color and a homey touch with these afghans. If the patient is cold, then it's a very practical gift as well. If the patient is too warm, it's placed at the foot of their bed.

Shari mentioned another very special aspect of this program. For families not going home with their loved ones, the afghan gives them a symbol of our sincere understanding while also providing a gift for them to keep and cherish. When she worked at another hospital as the perinatal chaplain, she learned how important this aspect was for the family. If they had lost their baby, they would not be going home with a warm little bundle. Their arms were tragically empty, so the gift of a bereavement blanket became vital. The act of giving the blanket helps to carve out and capture precious times and memories, made even more so because they are final. And at these times, the enclosed blessing card takes on special significance.

"God has this way of picking the blanket and leading us to the patient for whom it is intended, Shari explained. I can't tell you how many times Sister Barbara and I watch for the blue or dark blankets (for men) to come into the craft office. Then before we know it, the patient is here!"

Sometimes the patient isn't conscious, but a family member might say, "Oh, my grandmother used to knit and crochet. She would love this blanket! She knew this pattern and created many afghans using it." It is so psychologically helpful for the family members to see their loved one cared for in this way. They realize that quite often the hospital room (and therefore their family member) is cold. It gives the family great comfort seeing their loved one wrapped in warmth and caring.

Shari's favorite aspect of the program is being able to find an afghan in the patient's favorite color(s). She was with a patient, Janet, one day who was having a very hard time. Janet finally began to realize and accept that she wouldn't be getting better. As they sat talking, Shari mentioned the gifts provided for patients. She learned Janet's absolute favorite color was purple. Shari went to the volunteer office, and inside the cabinet was the most exquisite afghan, not just in purple, but in multiple shades of purple. "The whole family exclaimed as I spread it over her. Every time her husband saw me in the hospital corridors thereafter, he thanked me again and again. Hope was born, and this patient actually turned a corner and was able to go home. The question I can't help asking is, did the blanket as well as the love and caring it symbolized play a role in this patient's improvement?"

Shari's Personal Inspiration:

> "I used to make quilts with my mother, and we taught my aunt to sew by making a log cabin quilt. When my mother became ill, my aunt made *her* a log cabin quilt that Mom used during her illness. It was winter in Minnesota and my aunt finished the

quilt and sent it from her home in Montana to keep her sister warm and wrapped in love. I broke protocol in the Lutheran church at Mom's funeral by draping the quilt over her coffin. At the graveside, it was used to create a safe haven for Mom's youngest granddaughter (my daughter).

"These memories and my personal experiences keep me inspired to do this work. I know first-hand how powerful these gifts are and how they can provide healing in many forms, on many different levels. And now, as I'm making chemo caps and afghan squares during my commute, a new and very gratifying personal development has occurred. "Without saying a word to my daughter, she has decided she also wants to make chemo caps. I'm thrilled to be able to inspire a member of the younger generation to crochet, yes, but more importantly to embrace the concept of reaching out to others with love and caring."

10

Facing Death

The question is not how we will die, but how we will live.

– Joan Borysenko, PhD, American pioneer of integrative
medicine, author, and founding partner of
Mind/Body Health Science, LLC

L oss and the accompanying sadness are realities of
our lives. However, how we individually respond
in these situations is very personal. What follows is
a collection of experiences which illustrate the many
ways people approach their final days, issues and
concerns that affect them at this time, and the many
creative and inspired means that were utilized by the
staff and volunteers to bring contentment and peace to
the patients.

No One Dies Alone Comfort Companions

Our staff became aware of the No One Dies Alone program in 2009. Director of Volunteer Services Lillian Schonewolf, Spiritual Care Director Richard Brochu, and several others traveled to Pontiac, Michigan, for five days of intensive training. This program was founded by Sandra Clarke, a critical care nurse at Sacred Heart Medical Center in Eugene, Oregon, in 2002. Her intention was to provide the structure to enable hospital personnel and volunteers to be a loving presence at the bedside of those in the final hours of their lives. The program was further developed by Peg Nelson, a Nurse Practitioner/Palliative Care, at St Joseph Mercy Hospital, Pontiac, Michigan.

A team of twenty-five participated in the initial training at St. Mary. The group was composed of healthcare professionals and volunteers including doctors, nurses, nurse practitioners, social workers, spiritual counselors, volunteer comfort companions, volunteer staff, and Healing Environments volunteers.

The patient's doctors, palliative nurse and social worker, chaplain, and nursing staff taught and reviewed patient care and guided other staff and family with end-of-life concerns, in line with St. Mary's protocols for palliative and comfort care. With the family's permission, Comfort Companions could provide a loving presence for the patient at times the family couldn't be present. The family was assured that their loved one would always have someone with them.

The Comfort Companion prepared a peaceful environment—music, soft lighting, a warm afghan or blanket, prayers, or religious readings (based on the patient or family preference). Even when morphine was being administered and the patient was non-responsive, it is believed hearing is the last sense to be lost. Therefore, they would speak softly, hold the patient's hand, play music, or read to the patient. Though the Comfort Companion did not perform nursing duties, they were specially trained to observe the patient closely and alert the nurse if the patient was in pain, was restless, or if there were changes in breathing.

If the patient's family members were there, sometimes they wanted company too. The volunteers encouraged the family to talk about their loved one and to share a little bit about what made them the unique individual they were. As difficult as the final hours of life can be, Comfort Companions were there to provide support and to be that compassionate presence.

The No One Dies Alone Mission Statement

*We work together and with others to relieve suffering of mind,
body, and spirit, and to maintain the dignity
of every person touched by our care.*

— Elizabeth Kubler-Ross, Swiss-American psychiatrist,
pioneer in near-death experiences, and author

✝ St. Mary Medical Center

No One Dies Alone

St. Mary Medical Center
Program of Compassion and Love

The Healing Environments program through the Volunteer Department of St. Mary Medical Center is deeply devoted to providing comfort and compassionate care to our patients who are approaching end of life. Our No One Dies Alone (NODA) program is designed to ensure a loving presence in the patient's room, offering dignity and respect to our dying patients and peace of mind to their loved ones.

The No One Dies Alone program includes specially trained volunteers called Comfort Companions who visit with patients who have no one to be at their bedside or whose family members need to be away from the hospital for a period of time.

These volunteers are trained to assist in end-of-life care, and they visit the patient's room with the permission of the patient's family. Comfort Companions can provide family members and caregivers with much-needed relief and support.

St. Mary Comfort Companions prepare a peaceful, warm environment through music, a blanket, a prayer, or a gentle touch. During their visit, they read to the patient, hold the patient's hand, and recite from religious texts at the patient or family request. Comfort Companions honor the family's wishes regarding care and prayer.

Comfort Companions do not perform nursing duties, but they are trained to alert the nurse if the patient is in pain, is restless, or is in need of attention.

NODA Card

*

It Only Takes One to Forgive

One of the strongest choices you could possibly make as you seek healing is to let go of any unsolved anger you have toward others, as well as the fears that may contribute to your anger. When you don't forgive, you deny yourself a higher energetic payoff—as well as potential healing.

– *An Inside Job* by Susan Barbara Apollon,
American psychologist, and author

Angelo DeLorenzo is a certified Catholic chaplain, No One Dies Alone Comfort Companion, and harpist. Following four years of chaplaincy training, he received certification at the ripe young age of seventy-one.

Angelo accompanied Richard, Lil, and others to receive the training conducted by Peg Nelson. It was hoped that this program would provide answers to questions such as: How can we help people who have very few relatives or friends who are at end-of-life? If they do have relatives, possibly in distant parts of the country or abroad, when should they come? What of those who are estranged from family or don't have a community of friends? How can we significantly improve our care for those in the final stages of life and demonstrate more sensitivity for those in their inner circle?

Angelo was called to the bedside of a man who was very distraught, due to his estrangement from his children. This patient was ready to die, but he truly wanted to talk with his son and daughter to ask their forgiveness.

"I was a drunken fool, the patient told Angelo. I spent all our money on booze and left them penniless. I've lived a hard life, but I would still like to humbly apologize to them and ask for their mercy, though I know I don't deserve it."

Angelo offered to call this man's son, which he did, as he explained the situation and what was going on with his dad.

"Don't call him my dad; he was never a father to us! I'm not coming and *do not* call my sister; neither one of us wants anything to do with him!"

Angelo continued, "He would love to see you and ask for your forgiveness."

"Ain't gonna happen!" replied the son and he hung up.

The patient had been able to reach his brother who was on his way from Florida, and when he arrived, they were able to reconcile.

Angelo shared some wise council with this man. "It takes two to reconcile, but it only takes one to forgive. Maybe now, with a prayer, we can make that happen. Can you find it in your heart to forgive your daughter and son for not coming?"

"Yes," came his tearful reply. They prayed quietly together. Two days later he passed away with his brother by his side.

One experience proved to Angelo that this program was as much for the family as for the patient. The patient was lying still in the bed as his daughter sat beside him reading. Angelo was unaware that Jack hadn't spoken to his daughter Lisa, or anyone, in a week. Angelo started a conversation with Lisa when suddenly Jack looked at Angelo and asked, "Where are you from?"

"I'm from Philly but I'm working here."

"No, where are you from…originally?"

"Wisconsin."

"I can tell."

A twenty-minute conversation followed while Lisa sat amazed. Jack was finally able to admit to Lisa that he was in shock and denial caused by the diagnosis he had received and had withdrawn into himself. He was angry with life, angry with God, and angry with Lisa for not taking him out of the hospital. He appeared more at ease after venting his feelings. Angelo said his farewells and left father and daughter together.

As he walked down the corridor, Lisa came running out of the room saying, "Thank you, thank you! I am so grateful that you were there to help Dad open up. It means so much to me that he's communicating again and able to release those pent-up emotions."

Angelo also spent a night sitting at the bedside of an eighty-nine-year-old woman whose ninety-year-old husband needed company and support as he kept the vigil for his "Sweetheart." It was an honor to be present to offer solace and prayers for them both. The worst kind of isolation for those who are dying is not being able to say to people they love that they are going to die. If they wish to talk about death and do share, they transform from victims to the protagonist in their end-of-life story.

*

A Perfect Team

I've seen and met angels wearing the disguise of ordinary people, living ordinary lives.

– Tracy Chapman, American singer-songwriter

During our interview, Betty shared, "What a unique privilege it was to be called to this [No One Dies Alone] ministry. Having the opportunity to be with someone as they make their transition from this life to the next was an honor Nino and I share."

Betty was prepared for this work when her father, who had been her mother's caregiver during her struggle with Parkinson's and dementia, passed away. Betty brought her mother to her home where she and the family could care for her at night. During the day, caregivers were on site to attend to her mother's needs.

"Mom fell and broke her hip and had surgery at St. Mary. She didn't fully recover and had to be in a long-term nursing facility. Her health deteriorated and I sat at her bedside and prayed with her for many hours. She was readmitted to St. Mary, but it became clear that she wasn't going to recover. We were told she didn't have long to live. As I sat and prayed the rosary with her, one of the Sisters of St. Francis came in and asked if I would like some company. I accepted gladly and we continued to pray the rosary until Mom's gentle passing about an hour later. Through this experience, I was prepared to be able to comfort others as they passed."

Betty, Nino, and I reminisced about a NODA request we all shared in. I had received a call from the Intensive Care Unit requesting a No One Dies Alone volunteer to come to the bedside of Richard, an ICU patient who was near death from diabetic complications and other critical health issues. His family had said their goodbyes and the nurses didn't want him to be alone. I assured them I would have a Comfort Companion come as soon as possible, but I would stay with him until then.

I was able to reach Betty and Nino, who assured me they could get to the hospital within thirty minutes. I spoke with Richard's nurse to gather as much information about him as she could share. She confided she didn't expect him to live more than a few hours, but he was being kept comfortable. His religious preference was not listed in his file, but she thought reciting the psalms would be fine. I went to sit with Richard, introduced myself, and started quietly reading psalms and comforting texts.

Nino and Betty arrived shortly thereafter. Nino is blind and it wasn't easy for him and Betty to navigate the long corridors of the hospital. But they took their No One Dies Alone commitment very seriously and were devoted participants.

We stepped out and I quietly gave them the scant information I had about Richard. It was early afternoon and we agreed that I would check back with them in a couple of hours and update plans for him at that time.

When I returned, the scene that greeted me was absolutely beautiful. I stood silently in the doorway and appreciated Betty and Nino's calming presence as they lent an air of dignity to a difficult situation. They had drawn two chairs close together near Richard's bed and with their backs to the door, had created a loving prayer circle. Betty was gently stroking Richard's arm, thus assuring him that he was not alone. Nino and Betty's heads were angled toward one another as they quietly murmured psalms. Nino doesn't allow the fact that he is blind to interfere with volunteering. He has memorized many Bible passages.

The warm, loving spiritual essence surrounding them all was almost palpable. This state-of-the-art ICU suite, complete with all the requisite equipment, had been transformed into a haven of serenity and peace. I stood at the doorway and absorbed this beautiful scene and thought, "What a perfect team they are!" Richard made his transition shortly after, but drifted off very peacefully, surrounded by Betty and Nino's circle of love.

*

The Treasure Hunt

Happiness is a warm puppy.

– Charles Schultz, American cartoonist,
creator of "Peanuts"

Late one afternoon, Susie, the hospital chaplain for the oncology unit, dashed into my office with a special request. Julie, a young mother with terminal brain cancer, had just poured out her heart to Susie. Her doctor had just informed her she only had about seven more days of lucidity before she would need to be on a morphine drip to control the pain her cancer would cause. This young mother was heartbroken knowing she would never live to see her precious seven-year-old daughter, Megan, grow up. Not understanding what was happening to her mother, Megan had been begging for a puppy. Not exactly perfect timing…

Susie asked if we had *anything* with the image of a puppy or a stuffed dog in our Healing Environments stash. The happy answer was yes! We had a soft, cuddly fleece blanket, pure white with black paw prints all over it—think of all those dalmatians running wild on a white blanket of fleece snow!

Paw Prints

Susie was thrilled and we chatted while she patiently waited for me to take the photo, wrap the blanket, attach the blessing card, and seal the blanket in its plastic bag. With a hug, she was off to Julie with her "treasure."

The story continues…

Mary, Julie's nurse, had the idea the blanket could be hidden somewhere in Julie's room. When Megan arrived to visit her mom that evening, she could go on a "treasure hunt" to find her gift. After Julie composed a love note that was added, the package was secreted away. All was carried out according to plan and when Megan discovered her treasure, her "puppy," she squealed with delight and hopped up onto her mother's bed. After taking the soft blanket out of the bag, they snuggled together under it while reading the blanket blessing and Julie's love note to her daughter. The tears were coursing down Julie's face, a mixture of deep sorrow and sincere gratitude for Megan's happiness in the face of their dire circumstances.

These visits continued throughout the next week. Each night the blanket was hidden in a different spot in Julie's room and a new love note was added. Megan ran around the room looking everywhere to find where her puppy was hiding. She then snuggled in her mother's arms, hugging the blanket close, while they read that day's love note.

I don't know what their final night together was like, but what is clear is, even though this little girl is growing up without her mother, she has her "puppy," the memories of these few but special moments, and the deep and abiding love expressed by her devoted mother through her love notes—certainly a priceless treasure.

*

Memorial Day

Too often we underestimate the power of a touch, a smile, a kind word, a listening ear, or the smallest act of caring, all of which have the potential to turn a life around.

– Leo Buscaglia, American author, motivational speaker, and professor

It was the Friday before the Memorial Day weekend in 2010. Chris and Jean were my Healing Ambassadors and had taken the cart to the oncology unit. The crafters always work hard making red, white, and blue afghans prior to Memorial Day and Veterans Day.

We got a call requesting a visit to another unit where we were told a World War II vet lay close to death. Jean called me from the unit to ask if I could bring several of the veteran blankets to the patient's room. When I arrived, the man's daughter and daughter-in-law were at his bedside and speaking quietly with Jean and Chris.

His daughter was very emotional, and as tears filled her eyes, she told us about her strong, vibrant father, the rock of their family, who had received the Purple Heart for his valiant naval service. The tears could no longer be contained, and her sister-in-law held her as she wept. Though we didn't know him, we realized his death would be an enormous loss for this close, loving family.

We expressed our feelings of sadness and offered them the choice of three military blankets. His daughter chose a lovely large one and we spread it over her father. We all experienced the transformation that takes place when we perform this ritual; the energy in the patient's room is uplifted...by the colors, the textures, and not least by the outpouring of love and compassion expressed in each crafter's creation of a blanket designed to bring solace and feelings of peace.

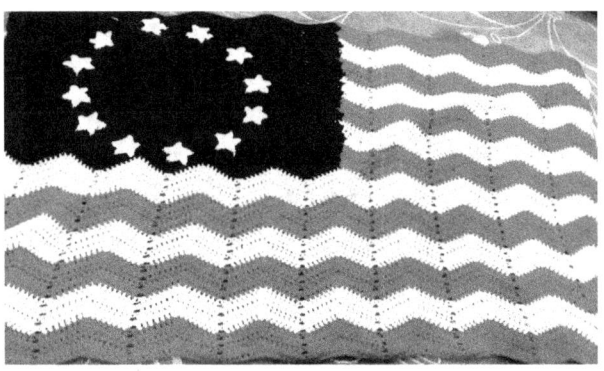

Crochet veteran flag blanket

As we joined hands and gathered to form a prayer circle around him, Chris recited the blessing. We remained connected for several minutes as we each offered our own prayers for this brave man, that his passing would be gentle, that he be received lovingly by God, and that his widow and family be granted the strength and grace to carry on.

They had been informed by his physicians that he only had a few days to live, and indeed, he died over the weekend. His wife was so distraught, she couldn't be there, but his daughter and other family members kept the bedside vigil. He passed peacefully, sheltered in his beautiful afghan, wrapped in the colors of the country he had fought to protect and defend.

Several weeks later, we received a heartfelt thank you card from the family. We learned that this veteran's grieving widow sleeps with the blanket each night, receiving solace from comforting herself in the folds of his afghan, the last thing to touch her beloved husband. In so doing, she continues to "connect" with him and feel his strength, energy, and love.

As Nancy Leporace, manager, Home Care and Hospice Volunteer Services at a local hospital wrote, "Life for a grieving person is forever changed and the task of adapting to this 'new normal' can be daunting. When we companion the grieving individual, we make room for all the emotions and challenges that accompany loss. This is often best done by active listening rather than by offering advice in an effort to 'move along' the bereaved. Grief does not follow a time-table pre-determined by others. Grief cannot be avoided or hurried along. 'Good grief' takes time!"

*

Unique Gifts

It is one of the most beautiful compensations of this life, that no one can sincerely try to help another without helping himself.

– Ralph Waldo Emerson, American essayist, lecturer, philosopher, and poet

Iris was in the first class of volunteers to be trained for the No One Dies Alone program. She felt especially humble and fortunate to be able to perform this ritual for the dying. Sometimes the patient's family was present also, and when this was the case, the experience was even more significant and meaningful for everyone.

A touching example of this occurred one evening. While she was sitting with Kay who was near death, the patient's son came in and soon his daughter joined him. As everyone introduced themselves, Iris asked him to tell her a little about his mother. He reminisced about some of their favorite times together, all of which centered around music, when he would play his guitar and sing to her. Iris asked if he had his guitar with him and was excited to learn that it was in his car. She encouraged him to bring it in, which he did. Iris was invited to experience an *amazing evening and unique family leave-taking.*

They closed the door and he and his daughter sang to his mom as he softly strummed his guitar. He played for quite a while, and Iris could see his mother's body relax more deeply. The love that came through the music was very moving, and Iris felt a level of intimacy created. She asked if they would prefer that she leave to give them private time together. They both said no, please stay.

Kay's son played his guitar for about ninety minutes. The nurse's aides came in to reposition Kay and the movement roused her. She looked up and saw her granddaughter. Kay looked as though she had seen an angel. The joy on her face was beautiful.

What a night. What a marvelous gift.

Iris is a hugger and a toucher, in fact, she's famous for her great hugs. As she sat with the patients, she held their hand, stroked their arm, spoke softly to them, read scriptures or psalms, and also sat quietly reading her own books. She observed the patient very closely for changes in their breathing and color. One day she was called to the bedside of a woman and told by the nurses that the patient's death was imminent. Iris pulled the chair close to the bed, held her hand, and spoke softly. As Iris watched her, the patient stopped breathing. Iris was just about to call the nurse when the nursing assistant came in to take the patient's blood pressure. Iris told her it wouldn't be necessary; the patient had just passed. Iris asked if the family was expected and was told they were waiting for the patient's son to arrive. She stayed at the bedside until he came.

While keeping the vigil for another patient, Iris was shocked when the patient suddenly sat straight up in bed, pointed over Iris's shoulder, and began speaking to "Harold." Iris didn't see Harold, nor could she decipher what the patient was saying, other than his name. But the patient was very focused, and then soon lay back down and relaxed. That was the only time Iris had ever witnessed someone communicating with a being not in our visual realm.

A beautiful leave-taking occurred when one of the nursing instructors was lying near death. Iris had been called to be there, even though many of the patient's nursing students had gathered to pay their respects and express their final goodbyes. The patient most definitely was not alone. In fact, Iris felt more like a cruise director as she kept the flow of visitors moving in and out of the patient's room. Sometimes, a few students would go in together, but some people requested privacy. Even though this obviously well-liked instructor was so close to death, there was also an undeniable sense of acceptance and almost of joy that her struggle with her disease was near an end. They obviously didn't want her to suffer any longer.

Iris confided to me that some of her friends wonder how she can do this work and actually find it rewarding. "I tell them I feel so blessed when I receive a NODA call. Each experience is a unique gift."

During the spring of 2001, my Father-in-Love received in-home hospice care from kind and dedicated caregivers. However, in mid-May he started having seizures and it was necessary to transfer him to Houston Medical Center Hospice, where he received wonderful care from "angels" disguised as hospice nurses. The family gathered and kept a constant vigil. On what would be his final day, I remember his last few minutes as if they occurred in slow motion.

We were watching his breathing very carefully. At one point, I glanced up to look outside. There, framed in the window was one pure white magnolia, blooming gloriously on the tree outside his room. I remember marveling at the perfection of nature.

Then I looked back at Sabah's still form. He had lost all of his beautiful red hair, lots of weight, and lay curled in the fetal position lightly covered by a sheet. He was only receiving oxygen, so there were no annoying mechanical sounds. Ron had made several music CDs of Sabah's favorites. At that moment, his and

Savtah's special song "Clare de Lune" started playing. I noticed Sabah exhale twice into his mask and then lay still. In that moment, his soulmate Savtah "came for him."

Savtah and Sabah

Also at that moment, our dear friend, Cantor Liz, gently pushed the door open and stepped in holding her beautiful golden-haired daughter in her arms. As tears streamed down my face, Liz drew me into her embrace. During our painful experience when Savtah had died following open-heart surgery two years prior and during Sabah's final months, Cantors Steve and Liz had been our steadfast spiritual supporters, lovingly guiding and caring for us during these most difficult trials.

We all drew more closely around his bed to say our final farewells. Following his nine-month battle, Sabah died peacefully and with dignity on that beautiful spring day in 2001.

No matter what he had endured on any given day, Sabah would always hug us good night and say, "*Thanks for a great day!*"

11

A Doctor's Deep Appreciation for the Volunteers

Is the volunteer program necessary in the hospital?
I think it's as vital as IV fluid!

– Dr. P, American internal medicine physician

This chapter contains one very significant contribution from a dedicated doctor who *loved* the Healing Environments Program and *everything* the volunteers did on behalf of the patients. As a house doctor, Doctor P was literally in every unit of the hospital. She witnessed the patients' suffering firsthand. Her sensitivity and insight will help heighten your awareness of the extent of the volunteers' effectiveness in soothing those who were suffering.

One cold and snowy winter day, Doctor P finally arrived at the hospital after a ninety-minute drive over slick roads. As she approached the elevator a volunteer stood there in her red jacket and gave the doctor a cheery hello. As they chatted, she mentioned her surprise at seeing the volunteer there at this time (nearly 7:00 p.m.) and in this weather. The volunteer, Paula, enthusiastically said how important this work was to her mental and emotional health, and that it "made her day" to be with those who might be in need of a little special care, a visit from someone non-medical who was there just for them.

Her words resonated with the doctor, because as she made her rounds through the hospital, Doctor P witnessed the outward expression of these sentiments many times as she observed the volunteers' generosity and altruism. "Many of my patients are feeling fear and anxiety, waiting for test results, facing surgery or some unknown new treatment. And the acts of kindness of the volunteers, sharing their own humanity and goodness to bring hope and inspiration to these patients is beautiful to witness. Those acts are priceless, and they don't even begin to describe the extent to which the volunteers share themselves so generously. They bring the 'other medicine' to the patients."

Her first encounter with the volunteers was when she was working in Same Day Surgery. There were quite a few miscarriages, and those young women, sometimes with their husband, partner, or a family member, but sometimes alone, were devastated. The life they had been carrying inside them was no more. They were at a crossroads of utter wretchedness. She found some printed brochures with helpful resource information, but these, though offering quality support, seemed cold, considering what these people were going through. She had seen the baby gifts made by the crafters for the newborns in the Mother and Baby Unit with handmade blessing cards attached. When she asked where these beautiful cards came from, she was directed to the volunteer office.

"Humanity is a bridge that builds itself from both ends, said Doctor P. Our patients' lives as they knew them are changed. The volunteers reach out to form that bridge to help the patients to their new existence. These handmade cards, so small, maybe three by four inches, became a strong connecting link for the families touched by grief.

"I walked into the volunteer office, stood at the entrance, and was amazed by the color and creativity 'happening' there. Crafters were making afghans at the table with brightly colored yarns spread out. Others were wrapping the cheerful blankets, preparing them to be taken to the patients. I spoke with Joan, the coordinator, about my specific requests regarding the baby cards, informing her of the recipients, and their special needs, considering what they would have been through.

"Because these patients had lost the baby, I asked that no cute little footprint or handprint stickers be on the cards. The doves, angels, butterflies, hearts, flowers, etc. that adorned many of the cards she showed me, would be fine.

"Joan listened attentively, and said she would get in touch with Peg, the artist, to pass along my request. Within a week, I had these very special cards for the young women. The nurses and I stored them in a special place where they could be easily accessed when needed. I felt that I had been present at the 'birth' of these cards. Simple as they are, the encouragement that is expressed is broad enough to cover many situations, bringing a heartfelt message of respect and caring."

Each card is unique, created by Peg H., but the wording is below.

For the family of a stillborn baby or miscarriage:

"May God, who understands each need,
Who listens to every prayer,
Bless you and keep you
In His tender loving care."

The volunteer office, and specifically, the Healing Environments group, became an amazing resource that Doctor P utilized frequently. She believes God gave the volunteers sunshine and courage as they brought their understanding, empathy, their inner strength to be in the patients' space at their moments of need. These unique individuals had the ability to be "in tune" with the patients' wide variety of moods, listened attentively and with deep sensitivity. They provided themselves as a "safe zone." They weren't coming in with any agenda. The patient was totally in charge of the visit, or they could choose to decline. It wasn't just the handmade gifts beautifully and thoughtfully created and generously given, but the volunteers themselves, also giving generously of their time, talents, and sincere desire to uplift the spirits of the patients, their fellow human beings.

Doctor P sometimes worked the seven p.m. shift, and might need an afghan, neck roll, or one of the other comfort items in the middle of the night. She would call the operators and ask them to have security meet her at the volunteer office. When the security guard let her in, she would get the keys to the cabinets, open the doors to what she thought of as an "art show-case," and select the needed items. The feeling that came over her time and again was like a kid in a candy store. The richness of the items the crafters had made was breathtaking. She felt it was a special blessing to be able to access these gifts at any time of the day or night, whenever they were required by the patients.

The Intensive Care Unit was one of the doctor's frequent stops. She was often present at the patient's bedside in the prayer circle when Sister Marie Barbara or one of the nurses would open and spread a hand-knit or crocheted afghan over a patient. This patient might be at the very end of their existence, fighting their final battle with their illness, as they saw their personhood vanishing. The afghans given to them were an expression of generosity and caring but were also a significant way of reaching out to let them know they had not been forgotten. As the beautiful blessing card was read to them, they might be too weak to respond in any dramatic way. But their eyes sometimes lit up or a small smile might cross their lips as their hand touched the soft folds of the blanket…and they knew, they felt, they were still recognized and respected. There is no IV infusion that can create that.

Doctor P felt these were some of the most treasured moments in the hospital setting, provided by the volunteer department, when a patient spent their final hours sheltered under one of the amazing handmade afghans. When the family gathered at their loved one's bedside, despite the grief they were feeling, there was still a sense of admiration for the workmanship and appreciation to the crafters working off-site who created these beautiful symbols of comfort. There was a certain joy as a family member pointed to the blanket and said, "Look what the volunteers made for Mom/Dad." Each one of these afghans was a work of art, the stitches, the colors and textures, the variety of designs, all worked together to infuse art into these items of comfort and the creativity is valued. Art transforms us and moves the soul.

Doctor P's dad was a Korean War veteran. On many occasions when he headed out, he proudly wore his hat. Quite often people would come up to him, thank him, and express their respect for him. As mentioned, the Veteran Appreciation Program initiated in 2015 provided excellent opportunities to honor and thank our veterans.

Sometimes on her rounds, she would learn that the patient she was visiting was a vet. If this person hadn't received his or her blanket yet, she would dash down to the volunteer office to get one. She always felt it to be a special honor to be able to take a few minutes to express her personal appreciation to the veterans for their service to our country, their deep commitment to ensure our freedom, and to safeguard our democracy. As she presented them with their blanket and the accompanying Appreciation Wristband, their eyes would shine with a quiet pride. An old soldier takes that pride to their grave.

St. Mary Medical Center is a Catholic hospital, but many faiths are represented throughout the patient population. The Spiritual Care providers endeavor to have people available to address the special needs of patients of other faiths. The chaplains and priests are some of the most-humble, beautifully soft-spoken "knights in God's armory." They are often dramatically in the middle of the most intense feelings, anger, sadness, unspeakable grief. They offer themselves as a gateway to opening a heart, to easing acute suffering. They have mentioned many times that the gifts of the volunteer crafters and the blessing card both help to ease the patients' and families' paths through difficult times.

"When people are suffering, in pain, just sad—we can't take it away," said Doctor P. "But we can be with them and respect them as fellow human beings. It has been a privilege to be able to utilize these special gifts from the volunteers to enable me to reach out to the patients in my care. But what makes them so much more valuable, is the gift of themselves, the crafters creating from home, the volunteers in the office wrapping and preparing the items to be given, the volunteers who take the items to the patients, all sharing their unique gifts, skills, generosity, and altruism.

To the marvelous volunteers, thank you:

"Thank you…for easing the pain of a gentleman's impending death, his pain and his family's pain, with the beautiful afghan you made. It gave him a sense of being cared for with respect and dignity at that point in his life's journey, the colors rendering back the warmth of life, even at that time.

"Thank you…for the neck roll pillow you made given to a patient nearly 100 years old. It made her feel that she had 'family' there when her family was very far away.

"Thank you…for sitting with someone who was anxious and afraid of overwhelming illness and being in the hospital, when they had no one.

"Thank you…for helping families who simply get lost in the hospital trying to find their loved one's room, while frightened and worried.

"Thank you…to so many pet therapists who lend themselves and their beloved, cute pets, large and small, to brighten lives and allow the patients to touch another of God's wonderful creatures. And thank you for also recognizing and stopping to give us (the staff) this therapy too, sensing our need as well as the patients'.

"For delivering a smile, a newspaper, a handshake, or simply a greeting… We thank you!

"We have said, what you do, ALL the things you do…they are treasures and a testament that are such an important part of a patient's care. We are fortunate and blessed to be on a team that YOU are ALL a part of.

"For your incredible dedication…day in and day out…good weather, rain and snow…we say sincerely…Thank YOU."

12

To Those We've Loved and Lost

> Do not stand at my grave and weep.
> I am not there. I do not sleep.
> I am a thousand winds that blow.
> I am the diamond glints on snow.
> I am the sunlight on ripened grain.
> I am the gentle autumn rain.
> When you awaken in the morning's hush
> I am the swift uplifting rush
> Of quiet birds in circled flight.
> I am the soft stars that shine at night.
> Do not stand at my grave and cry.
> I am not there. I did not die.

– Mary Elizabeth Frye, American poet and florist

Death is a reality of life, we know that. But I always felt deep sorrow when one of our volunteers died. They each brought their own unique "something" to their work. Their devotion touched my heart. They might tell me, "I don't schedule anything on Tuesday. Tuesday is my St. Mary day."

I'd like to introduce you to some of these wonderfully dedicated women who passed during my nine years as coordinator and manager of the program. I'd also like to express my sincere appreciation to their loved ones who shared the details which enrich these stories.

*

Living Her Dream

Love what you do and do what you love. Don't listen to anyone else who tells you not to do it. You do what you want, what you love. Imagination should be the center of your life.

– Ray Bradbury, American author, and screenwriter

Ruth always dreamed of being a nurse, but her father discouraged this path, and instead she attended secretarial school. However, her husband died when she was only fifty-five years old, so when her children were grown, she made a commitment to use her days and time wisely, doing for others.

After her husband's death, Ruth received a condolence card with a poem by Helen Steiner Rice, which she adopted as her way of living through her sorrow.

Her family found it folded in her purse after she passed. It advised her not to fill her days with tears and sorrow but with purposeful deeds…and she did.

She brought her beautiful smile and innate comforting ways to the patients at St. Mary. Fortunately, at that time, volunteers were able to work three days a week at the hospital. Also, Ruth's ideal position was available, that of "Care Mate." Volunteers serving in this capacity were specially trained to perform many of the duties nurses' aides do today. They were able to help feed, bathe, dress, and move the patients. Additionally, as a volunteer, she was able to just sit and visit with a patient, especially those who had few or no visitors, or who were anxious about their condition, treatment, or who just needed to talk.

When the No One Dies Alone program was introduced at St. Mary in 2009, Ruth was in the first group of volunteers to receive the training to become a Comfort Companion. This position was certainly not for everyone, but for those who were interested, they performed a magnificent service for patients at their end of life. For Ruth, providing companionship and a loving presence to those approaching their final hours became one of her most meaningful and memorable services at the hospital.

Ruth approached the end of her own life with definite ideas of how she wanted things to be conducted. At the age of ninety-three, she was diagnosed with cancer, and though given options to prolong her life, she chose quality of days over quantity. She wanted to enjoy the time she had, feeling as good as she could. She continued to volunteer at St. Mary, but was there only on Thursdays, "her day."

When I spoke with her daughter, Linda, she graciously shared these details about Ruth's final days. "We could see Mom was getting weaker, but she kept going and never wanted to miss 'her Thursdays' at the hospital. In fact, she volunteered the week before she died. "Then, on *that* morning, I had heard Mom moving around in her room and then things got quiet. I went to check on her and to ask if she was ready to have breakfast. I found her on the floor beside her bed. I immediately called 911, knelt close, and assured her we were getting help."

The paramedics arrived quickly and got Ruthie into the ambulance. Linda was able to ride with them. She called her brother to have him meet them at St. Mary Emergency Room. As the ambulance driver and his companion were unloading Ruth from the ambulance, he started laughing. Linda looked at him quizzically and he said, "Honest to goodness, your mom just gave me the biggest smile I've ever received."

Linda replied, "I think it's because she knows where she is, her 'home-away-from-home,' and she's just so happy about that!

"In the ER, she was taken for an MRI, but when this very kind doctor came to speak with us, he said that Mom had suffered a severe stroke. He informed us that we could request a neurological consult, but there was no way Mom would be able to maintain a full life. The doctor informed us that we had a major decision to make.

"I said, 'Actually we don't, because my mom has written very specific detailed instructions.'"

The doctor requested to see what she'd written. As he started to read her words, this very professional man began to *laugh*. He apologized, saying, "I am so sorry, but I have never in all my years of practice experienced anyone who was so adamant about what she does and does NOT want done! Your mother has given you the best gift in the world, by taking this burden off your shoulders." Even in the midst of this terrible news, Ruth had reached out to give her family comfort.

"Mom lingered for several days, but my brother and I divided the vigil so that one of us was always with her, Linda tearfully confided. I kept apologizing to her, saying I was sorry I couldn't do this work as well as she had. The volunteers were able to come to visit and pay their respects. Her room was happily filled with these friends she had known through her years of volunteering and her church companions as well. Everyone was sharing favorite 'Ruthie Stories.' As difficult as it was for us to have her linger, it was a blessing for the volunteers who knew and loved her to have this opportunity to say their personal farewells. And my brother and I were also blessed to be able to meet so many of her fellow volunteers."

Ruth passed on her day, Thursday, in one of the hospice rooms on the oncology unit where she had kept many vigils for others. She was also being lovingly attended by one of the nurses with whom she had worked for so many years. Linda and I both felt Ruth was orchestrating events right until the end. The reason we believed this is that she had a steady stream of Thursday volunteers visiting throughout the day until 2:00 p.m., the time the volunteers leave to go home. Ruth passed shortly thereafter.

"Mom also had very specific directives for her funeral. She wanted only family at the service, graveside, and back at home. She realized many of her fellow volunteers, St. Mary staff, and friends would be hurt by this desire, so she actually went around the hospital preparing them so they wouldn't feel they were personally being left out.

"She loved Brother's Pizza, so that's what we served to the family following the service. She had also made many photo albums during her life. These were especially wonderful for her grandchildren and great-grandchildren to be able to glimpse what life was like 'way back when.' Looking through the albums together brought Mom right into the family room with us. Everyone was reminiscing, laughing, and sharing Ruth."

*

Renaissance Woman

This world belongs to the enthusiast!

– Ralph Waldo Emerson, American philosopher,
essayist, and poet

Vicki and the love of her life, partner, and best friend Tom, were married for thirty-four years. They were teachers of literature at Holy Family University and at LaSalle University. Vicki also taught in the Philadelphia Catholic schools. A student of the piano and violin, she also thoroughly enjoyed her role as choir master at the Shrine of Our Lady of Czestochowa in Doylestown, PA. She was beloved by her students and was always surrounded by a host of friends who enriched her life.

When she and Tom weren't traveling the world together, she filled her life with charitable works. She devotedly worked with the Benedictine Monks of Still River, Massachusetts, visited St Padre Pio's Center weekly. She published poetry and was senior proofreader for Holy Family University's literary journal, Folio.

Tom spoke with love and admiration about her.

"Victoria was an exceptional person, her life spread out across a multitude of landscapes, a kind of Renaissance figure, capable of creating one thing, then preparing another, then on and on. For instance, as a writer (both scholarly and creatively), she earned a bachelor's degree at Holy Family University and a master's degree at Villanova, taught English in parochial schools of Philadelphia, to name just a few of her educational accomplishments. She was a marvelous pianist, sang in the choir of the Shrine of Our Lady of Czestochowa, and became the choirmaster for five years. She also entertained her family, friends, and students as she played the violin for them. She was a woman of many talents, to be sure."

Victoria never did anything halfway. We were so fortunate to count her as one of our more than 300 crafters. In the two years she was able to work with us, she contributed over 1,200 hours making absolutely beautiful comfort items for our patients. She would arrive at our monthly meetings with two large bags filled with her latest creations. Vicki challenged us all (in the nicest possible ways) by frequently using new patterns for her afghans or shawls and offering to teach us the pattern. She "wowed" us as she drew the beautiful creations from her bag and would say, "This is a pattern I recently found, but it's really easy; you just…" Well, they weren't always easy, but they *were* always beautiful and meticulously made, imbued with prayers and blessings for the recipient in Vicki's unique way of uniting the sacred with daily activities. She constantly encouraged us to reach higher, do more, be better, and try new things. As Vicki's husband said, she loved staying purposeful, even as her health declined. Crocheting and creating her meticulous afghans helped give her serenity, knowing they would benefit those in need.

She also introduced the crafters to the hat looms that enabled us to greatly increase the number of winter hats we made, not only for our patients but also for the homeless of our community.

Dear Vicki,

We who knew and loved you in this life, remember and miss you so much! You brought such *"Joie de Vivre"* and your own personal brand of living to each day. We remember your energy, enthusiasm, and the brilliance you brought to everything you touched. We hope you're up in Heaven, helping to make it even more beautiful!

*

Talented Hands

The world is but a canvas to our imagination.

– Henry David Thoreau, American essayist,
poet, and philosopher

Connie Lombardi (Tom's sister) was a sweet and diminutive lady who created unique soft dolls and "critters" for our patients of all ages. And she did this using only scraps and small bits of left-over lace, ribbon, fabric, yarn, and stuffing. She would then embellish them with a touch of delicate embroidery, her "signature." Each was a one-of-a-kind creation made with love. Her eye for color and detail was amazing.

She and I had great times together in my office. I would call her immediately when we received a donation of "bits and pieces," her "treasures." When she arrived, we would take everything out of the box or bag as she spread it across the table. Suddenly she'd be putting this piece of lace with that bit of fabric and creating before my eyes, as a happy smile spread across her lovely face. She had been given an amazing gift from God, and using this ability brought her such joy, sharing it with others, even more. The crafters loved to set aside these odds and ends for Connie, because they knew nothing would go to waste, and wonderful creations would be the happy result.

The patients were often so touched and intrigued by the work of her hands as they inspected the details. Each doll face was given a different expression, as well as eye and hair color. Her animals were fanciful, whimsical, fantastical creations that delighted the eye.

Connie also taught rosary making to several groups of volunteers at the hospital. These were carried to the patients on our Healing Carts and offered as gifts by the Healing Ambassadors and the chaplains, who blessed these items prior to distribution.

Connie, I hope you're having fun in Heaven making everything more beautiful.

*

My Mom Irene, My Crafting Partner

You are the captain of your ship.
You're steering your path where you want to go.

– Irene R. Golden, daughter, wife, sister, mother, grandmother, crafter, and amazing human being

Celeste and her mom, Irene, were unique. They were one of three mother/daughter teams of Healing Environments crafters. Celeste and I enjoyed a wonderful "walk down memory lane" as she shared anecdotes, family stories, idiosyncrasies, and gave us this beautiful tribute filled with insights of her beloved mother.

Celeste's mom was the youngest of seven children, born to a tailor from Eastern Europe, who had come to America to provide his family with a better life. Money was always tight, but they found joy in simple things, listening to stories, or playing in the park.

An extra special treat was an ice-cream cone.

"Mom always had a way with people, Celeste proudly stated. She could make them laugh, tell jokes, or just be there to listen." Life was hard raising Irene and her siblings. Her dad fought in WWII, serving in Germany where he earned a number of medals. However, he returned with what is now known as Post Traumatic Stress Disorder. He was forever changed and became an alcoholic. When he was at home, everyone tried to be as quiet as possible, because loud noises would always startle him, which led to angry outbursts. Irene's mother protected them if they forgot and set him off.

Crocheting was always an outlet for Irene, and provided a "calm in the storms," a source of enjoyment, and a means of expressing her creativity. She made practical and beautiful garments and decorative items. She made Celeste, her sisters, and their friends unique sweaters. Her work was so admired for its beautiful detailing that she was frequently asked to make baby items for members of her parish, friends, and family members. Sometimes total strangers would see her work, admire it, and she would offer to make something for them.

When Celeste was in high school, she asked her mom to teach her to crochet. Irene happily agreed, though her patience was definitely tried by Celeste's initial trial and error efforts. They both persevered and were able to enjoy many years crocheting together.

Irene was also a great seamstress and often made matching dresses for Celeste and her sisters. (For some reason, their brothers weren't interested.) She sewed curtains and other decorative items for the family's home. She had a green parrot named Birdee and even sewed the cover for his cage. She loved to spoil him, cooking his favorite veggies and treats. One of their special morning activities was sharing grapefruit.

One of Irene's favorite pastimes was going antiquing with her daughter Karen, an avid antique doll collector. Irene sewed many beautiful dresses and gowns and crocheted accessories for the dolls. She wasn't particularly interested in collecting herself, until she admired a pin collection on one trip. That's when she "got the bug" to start collecting—antique bug pins to be exact! Beautifully detailed insects made of cloisonné, metals encrusted with jewels, painted wood, and other materials started filling special display boxes in her home.

In 2010, Irene and Celeste learned about the Healing Environments Program at St. Mary. They decided that participating would be a great way to give back to their community. They made many beautiful afghans, but eventually, the weight of a full-size afghan became too heavy and cumbersome for Irene to handle. As she sought other patterns, something unique to offer, "Irene's Capelets" came into being and soon became one of the patients' favorite items. They sat comfortably on the shoulders without slipping and had a lovely roll collar to keep the patients' necks warm. Irene and Celeste attended many monthly craft meetings at St. Mary, and always enjoyed the camaraderie of the group.

Irene's Capelet

On October 3, 2015, the family took Irene on a cruise to celebrate her ninetieth birthday. All the guests were hiding just inside the ship at the foot of the gang plank. The captain escorted her to the entrance where everyone jumped up, yelling, "Surprise!" They all enjoyed a wonderful catered meal including many of her favorites (especially crab cakes…she was an avid crabber). When the multi-tiered birthday cake was wheeled in, she gave a speech telling everyone how grateful she was for the gift of living these ninety years, how much she had enjoyed the blessing of having all of them in her life, and giving thanks for their love and devotion.

Two weeks later, she started complaining about not feeling well. The family was alarmed because it was very rare for her to have any complaints. She felt so weak that they went to the ER. During the exam, the nurse required a urine sample, and though she drank liters of water, she wasn't able to comply. She was admitted to the hospital to determine the cause, and she was found to have a blood disorder.

Her doctor recommended she see a specialist at St. Mary, who told her she had a very aggressive form of leukemia. Mom wanted to know "the bottom line…how long do I have?" He estimated three to six months. He started presenting treatment options, which wouldn't be a cure, but could prolong her time. She wanted nothing to do with that. He then started discussing hospice possibilities. "She chose to stay at my home, have home hospice, which proved to be a true blessing. She was comfortable in her familiar surroundings and the hospice staff was amazing, very caring and kind. Celeste and other family members were always at hand in the house to keep her company," Celeste said.

In mid-November, the weakness became more pronounced. A hospital bed was set up on the ground floor, and Irene received many visitors there. She was able to use this precious time to visit with each family member individually to say farewells, impart special messages to each, and secure closure.

Irene was a great planner and had very firm ideas about her "arrangements." She was very clear about her desires, which helped the family to comply with her wishes. Although she had many friends and knew scores of people who loved and admired her, she wanted just a small gathering for the cremation service but did not want to be interred.

"I love nature, sprinkle me in nature," Irene said.

She didn't have much appetite as December 2015 went on, but a couple of weeks before Christmas, she said she'd like something special to eat. Celeste was so excited, anticipating she would be able to make one of her mother's favorite dishes. She asked, "Ok Mom, what would you like?"

Irene's response came back, "Chicken broth." No, she didn't want any chicken or veggies, just the broth, which at that point was comfort food.

Two days before Christmas Eve, the hospice nurse suggested administering the morphine that had been prescribed if Irene required it, knowing her pain would escalate. She wasn't ready for that, but she was slipping in and out of consciousness. "Santa" came to visit her (my husband donned the suit and bought a beautiful long white beard). She wasn't quite "with it" and actually seemed to think he *was* Santa. She asked where he'd left his reindeer. He replied they were out in the front yard and were just fine. She thanked him for coming; she was always so appreciative.

Celeste spoke lovingly about her mom's final days. "Mom had predicted she would 'go' on Christmas Eve. She had spoken with all of us about this and apologized, not wanting to spoil future Christmases for the family. We all concluded that it would actually be a gift, a fitting time to remember her when we were all gathered together…and that's the way it was. She passed early that Christmas morning in 2015, just as she planned."

*

My Catherine – She Could Make Anything!

So now faith, hope and love abide, these three;
but the greatest of these is love.

– 1 Corinthians 13:13

"When I first met Catherine, she was eighteen, her loving husband Tony said. We married in our early twenties, and by then she had fallen in love with sewing…as well as with me! Her aunt could look at a person and make them a dress perfectly fitted to them. She made Catherine's beautiful wedding gown…using no pattern. My mother was a professional seamstress, and the three of them had great times together. The first year we were married, I bought Catherine her first sewing machine, a Singer, which I still have."

As their children came along, she sewed their clothes and dresses for herself. She also sewed draperies, pillows, and tablecloths for their home. She was a homemaker in the best sense of the word. In addition to sewing, she loved to cook and experiment with new recipes. At one point she took a cake decorating course and started making beautiful cake creations for a local bakery. "She would decide to do something, and she did."

Years later she heard about the Healing Environments Program. By that time, she owned five sewing machines, one of which was a quilting machine. When she came to my office one Tuesday morning, she brought several items to give us an idea of her versatility. She spread out a beautiful lap quilt with intricate swirling stitches. She also brought an afghan, which she was still in the process of completing. As we talked, and I told her more about the program and its purpose, she crocheted the blanket, never looking down at her hands. I was so intrigued by the complex design and asked if she had a pattern for it. She did not. In fact, she said she *never* used patterns.

Catherine was also an accomplished knitter. She knit baby ensembles (blanket, booties, and caps) and gave them to the newborn nurseries at two local hospitals. She never wasted time.

Beaming, Tony said, "If she had ten minutes, she'd sit at one of the machines and sew something, or work on a crochet project. She was a really great person, always doing things for others. We had a lot of fun living life together. She was deeply committed to our family. Her grandchildren have had a tough time accepting her death. Every morning while looking at her photo, I tell her how much I miss her."

*

Aunt Betty

I think everybody needs a passion. Whether it's one passion or a hundred, that's what keeps life interesting.

– Betty White, American actress, comedian,
author, and animal rights advocate

Aunt Betty, what a wonderful sense of color she possessed. Bright and sunny yellow was her favorite hue, which matched her cheerful disposition and was quite often included in her creations. She, like Vicki, enjoyed challenging herself with complex crochet patterns. When I knew her, she was in her eighties and invited everyone to call her Aunt Betty. She was confined to a wheelchair in her later years but used her time generously to make items for others. She usually contributed four to six afghans a month to St. Mary. We used a "relay system" to get the afghans from her home to the hospital. Her niece, Lynne, would take the afghans to church the following Sunday and would then give them to one of our volunteers, Annie (also a member of her church).

Annie brought them to my office where we would exchange the blankets for more yarn for Betty, and the process was reversed. Aunt Betty also made prayer shawls for church congregants, blankets, scarves, and hats for the homeless and anyone in the community who was in need or going through tough times.

Lynne's mother died when she and her twin brother were nine years old. Aunt Betty and Uncle Russ took them and their older sister in and raised them as their own. Lynne told me how very loving her aunt was.

"She was like a second mother to me, Lynne said. She was always helping people in the community as well. She was a natural organizer and knew how to get things done. She had worked for GE for many years. Betty dealt with difficulties in a straight-forward manner. She was a 'Take charge, tough love, make it happen' strong woman who set a marvelous example that continues to guide our family."

*

"The Gails"

Our generation has the ability and the responsibility to make our ever-more connected world a more hopeful, stable, and peaceful place.

– Natalie Portman, Israeli-born American actress, director, and producer

"The Gails" were one of the first five teams of Healing Ambassadors. They were a complementary pair. Gail

B was very jovial and spirited. Gail G was quieter and brought a lovely air of calm and serenity to the patients. When I happened to be on the oncology unit during their rounds, quite often I would find them laughing with a patient and visitors as they lightened the mood with their special brand of cheer. Both "Gails" had previously suffered with cancer themselves, a fact which further cemented their bond *and* drew them to this work. They chose to focus their service to alleviate the suffering of others experiencing the same illness. We were deeply saddened when Gail B's cancer returned, and she died several months after.

Gail's first love was serving others, and following graduation from Southeast Missouri State University, she became an elementary school teacher. Thank you, Gail, for your great spirit, determination, and sense of humor that you never lost. As her beloved Charlie said of her at her memorial, "We celebrate a wonderful woman who, whether she realized it or not, dedicated herself to being of service to others. Would that all of us could be as fortunate to be able to say that when our day comes to say goodbye."

*

Brooklyn Helen

The meaning of life is to find your gift. The purpose of life is to give it away.

– William Shakespeare, English playwright, poet, and actor

Yes, the work of one of our crafters came all the way from Brooklyn, NY. How did this happen, you might ask? Helen's daughter Wendy lived relatively near the hospital. She went to visit her mom in the city every other weekend. Wendy's sister went on the other weekends. Helen was a crochet enthusiast, and when Wendy told her about our program, Helen excitedly offered to participate. She made the most beautiful baby and children's sweaters with matching caps. Wendy would take the yarn we provided for our crafters to Brooklyn and several weeks later, four or five sweater sets would appear.

Helen's Sweater & Cap Set

I spoke with Helen by phone periodically, and she frequently mentioned the pleasure she received from imagining the "little people" who would be warm and cozy wearing her items. She never failed to thank us for providing this work that kept her days purposeful, her hands busy with meaningful labor, and her mind off her aches and pains.

*

Camille

If you want to touch the past, touch a rock. If you want to touch the present, touch a flower. If you want to touch the future, touch a life.

– Author Unknown

Teacher, Eucharistic minister, and talented seamstress, Camille had a special gift for encouraging others. In her professional life, she taught special needs children and went on to study "Hands-on Science" techniques for kindergarten through third grade. She brought many innovative ideas for hands-on science projects to her young students at Sol Feinstone Elementary School. She also initiated a successful science fair at the school.

Camille and her husband Bill lived in an over fifty-five community where she "encouraged" many friends and neighbors to help make neck roll pillows for the patients at St. Mary. Having been a patient there herself on multiple occasions, she realized first-hand the comfort a neck roll pillow could provide.

She was an enthusiastic "cheerleader" for our program and wouldn't take no for an answer. If the friend didn't sew, she taught them how to stuff the pillows. If they could hand sew, she showed them how to stitch the seam closed. If they had a sewing machine, they were given fabric and the pattern for the neck rolls. When we introduced the Veteran Appreciation Program, she and her friends made hundreds of neck rolls using fabric imprinted with stars, stripes, and flags. Toward the end of Camille's life, the group would meet at her home to make it more convenient for her, and Bill brought the finished items to my office.

Camille never wasted anything. She saved scraps of fabric from her many sewing projects and used them to make cheerful "crazy quilts" for the patients. These were a favorite with men especially, perhaps because the colors and patterns were vibrant and bold. She sometimes gave us one to sell at the craft sales. Her charming and cheerful creations always attracted quite a lot of attention…and brought a good price!

Dear Camille, we know you're "up there" spreading beauty everywhere.

*

Ruth

The purpose of life is not to be happy, but to matter—to be productive, to be useful, to have it make some difference that you have lived at all.

– Leo Rosten, American humorist

Following retirement from her extensive teaching career, Ruth was seldom seen without knitting needles in her hands, unless she was sewing or reading with her grandchildren and great-grandchildren. She was known for her creativity and liveliness, her strength and courage in the face of adversity, her charming sense of humor and fun-loving personality, and for taking time for others.

In later years, Ruth and her husband wintered in Florida. Prior to their drive south, she would come to my office to receive several large bags of yarn that she took with her, her "stash" for the winter. In the spring, she returned with the ten to twelve unique afghans she had made during the previous months.

Thank you, Ruth, for your devotion to our patients as you shared your talents and gave so generously. Thanks also for the gift of your beautiful smile and warmth.

Author's Note:

The list above includes the volunteers associated with the Healing Environments Program who passed away during the nine years I coordinated the program of whom I was aware. To the families and friends of others who died about whom I did not know, please accept my heartfelt apologies. May their memories be a blessing.

13

Taking Action

Nothing is impossible, the word itself says "I'm possible!"

– Audrey Hepburn, British actress, fashion icon,
and humanitarian

I t is my sincere hope that you have enjoyed reading these stories and sharing our many experiences.
Now perhaps you have a keen desire to make a difference in your own life. I've listed a number of ideas and
helpful contact and resource information to assist you
in accomplishing your goals and perhaps implement-
ing new ideas in your own community.

As I write this, we are in the seventh month of the
coronavirus pandemic, August 2020. During these
incredibly stressful times, when so many news reports
are understandably focused on tragic events, there is
a desire to balance these facts with intentional good
deeds and our own acts of kindness, *to do what we can*

where we are. We hear of these devastating occurrences and may feel helpless, wondering how we can possibly make an impact and reach out. Crafters often answer the needs of friends or their communities by springing into action to make things.

An example of this is "Mask-Making Frenzy," which was created in March, when the Sacramento chapter of the American Sewing Guild learned of a dire need for masks and protective equipment for the medical professionals at their local hospitals. As a national organization, members of roughly 130 ASG chapters around the country have made millions of masks as well as protective garments for medical professionals in their communities and have shipped them to those cities experiencing the highest number of cases.

Wilma's Masks – 3 of 17,000

Staying purposeful in our lives is so vital to being involved, mentally alert, and to sending our good out into the world. If you **knit, crochet, sew, or create other crafted items,** think about giving at least a few to a local organization—hospitals, senior centers, assisted living and hospice centers—or to someone you know who is experiencing tough times, struggling to make ends meet. You may not know that person well, but a simple, seemingly small act of kindness can be significant to them.

For example, a winter scarf, hat or some other quickly made item can make a huge difference for someone who can't afford to buy these items. Many religious organizations have crafting groups that make much-needed items for members of their congregations and for the homeless. And it's not necessary to be a member of the organization to participate.

Don't craft or have "a creative bone in your body?" Any craft group would happily receive a gift card to a craft store for the purchase of yarn, fabric, and other supplies.

Donating to or helping at your **local food kitchen or pantry** is another great way to reach out. These facilities are in direct contact with the homeless of any community. Maybe you've heard about a neighbor who is ill or who has lost a loved one. Making a meal for them, offering to do errands, or driving them to an appointment could give them a much-needed lift. Just listening and letting them know they're not alone can add a positive note to their day.

Below is the list of the positions and programs aligned with the Healing Environments Program, as well as contact information for specific organizations. To locate crafting groups in your community, check craft and yarn stores, religious organizations, senior centers, senior daycare, and community facilities that usually organize groups or check online. Additional resources mentioned throughout the book can be found in Appendix III.

Volunteer positions at healthcare facilities require specialized training provided by staff. During the COVID-19 pandemic, these sessions have been suspended for everyone's safety. But don't allow this hiatus to deter you. Stay in touch with the volunteer department periodically, informing them of your desire to be contacted for training when it again becomes available. If you can, complete the volunteer application, being sure to mention the specific type(s) of position that would interest you. They'll be interested in your talents, education, and experience (both professional and personal) that would make you a good "fit" for the position. They may even have interim suggestions for work that can be completed by volunteers off-site during this challenging time.

We know the pandemic is causing a great deal of stress for our healthcare providers all over the country.

We send them our heartfelt appreciation for their brave efforts and the long hours they devote, despite shortages of personal protective garments, ventilators, and additional equipment.

Challah and Shabbat Visitors – For Jewish patients, these services help to provide a sense of normalcy and the ability to welcome the Sabbath, despite hospital confinement. Contact local synagogues, The Jewish Federation, or Jewish Family Services to find out if such a program exists in your area…or start one.

Clown Therapy – specially trained clown therapists provide light-hearted visits to people in waiting rooms, pre-op areas, and many units.

Courses are available online.

Eucharistic Ministers – volunteers visit with and offer the sacraments to patients throughout the hospital (overseen at St. Mary by the Spiritual Care Department).

Healing Ambassadors – volunteers visit seriously ill patients, offering gifts of comfort items, and spending time with them to bring a pleasant distraction to their day. This work requires the ability to be with sick patients. Many of our Healing Ambassadors had either endured illness themselves or with close relatives. Retired nurses were also drawn to this position. Having been in similar situations provided the experience needed to approach this work with confidence and often a desire to give back.

Life Story Writers – Volunteers interested in communicating with patients to capture their experiences and, based on the information gathered, create life story boards. (The person being interviewed does not need to be near death or in a healthcare facility.) Writing skills and/or crafting skills are helpful but not essential. These interviews can also be recorded on a mobile device with the person's permission. (A signed permission form is essential.). In the hospital we provided a consent form we asked the patient or family member to sign.

Music Ambassadors – Individuals or choral groups perform on a scheduled basis or occasionally. These positions do not require entering patients' rooms.

No One Dies Alone – "'Comfort Companions'" were specially trained to sit at the bedside of dying patients and, comfort and hold vigil in their final hours (many had experienced previous bedside vigils with family or friends). Each volunteer provided the staff with days and times of their availability. Check sites online.

Pet Therapy – specially trained dogs and their owners visit many units and surgical waiting rooms throughout the hospital. To research certification in your area, check online for such organizations as Therapy Dogs International, Therapy Dogs Inc., Pet Partners (certifies cats and other pets as well as dogs), Love on a Leash, American Service Pets.

Respite Companions – volunteers available for extended visits with patients (not dying) experiencing stress and anxiety, or to spend time with those who had few or no visitors. Ease with conversation and good listening skills are helpful.

Veteran Appreciation Program – veteran volunteers deliver red, white, and blue fleece blankets, thank the veterans for their service to our country, and spend quality time with these patients and their families, if present. Crafters made handtied fleece blankets (imprinted with military designs) presented to in-patient veterans and active-duty military. No sewing necessary. Instructions are available. www.YouTube.com DIY No Sew Fleece Blanket Tutorial

VA Hospitals would greatly appreciate blankets for their patients.

WOMENHEART – National Program brought to St. Mary. Women living with cardiac issues visit newly diagnosed female patients providing information, understanding, and support. Check your area for local programs or contact www.womenheart.org.

Zipper Club – visits by volunteers living with cardiac issues to those who have undergone open-heart or other heart-related surgery. Learn more at www.zipper-club.net.

The definition of a volunteer is one who offers to do something to benefit another person, group, or organization, without the expectation of receiving anything in return. Acts of altruism and kindness can be wonderfully inspiring for the giver as well as those receiving. I can't tell you how many times one of our volunteers would return to the office from their rounds and tell me how richly satisfying this work was for them.

We are all interconnected. That fact has been made abundantly clear by what our entire world is experiencing as we fight the COVID-19 virus. We *can* make a difference. The things we do don't have to be monumental. It is so often what we would consider a *little thing* that can make a *BIG difference* for someone else.

The only gift is a portion of thyself. The poet brings his poem; the shepherd brings his lamb…the girl, a handkerchief of her own sewing.

– Ralph Waldo Emerson, American essayist, lecturer, philosopher, and poet

Joan Portman, American author, keynote speaker, trainer, consultant, crochet enthusiast, and Founder, Healing Environments, LLC
Email: joan@joanportman.com
Website: www.joanportman.com
Founding Member, One Hundred Most Powerful Women, OneWoman.ca

If you have a story you feel could benefit others, I invite you to share a brief summary in the "Contact" section of my website in the message box.

To hear an interview with Joan, conducted by lawyer Yvette E. Taylor, Esquire, go to her podcast at ythlaw.com, scroll down to the bottom of the homepage and click on "What's Your Legacy?" Enter "Joan Portman: Creating Healing Environments, November 1, 2018" in the search listing.

Joan was also a keynote speaker at the OneWoman.ca – Born to be Powerful Global Summit, Sunday, June 13, 2021. Available on the OneWoman Facebook page.

Acknowledgements

While the creation and daily operation of the Healing Environments Program required the loving energy of many people within our community, it is not possible to recognize everyone in this book. Please know, however, that I am deeply and sincerely appreciative of *all* you did to sustain and grow this program. Your participation, whatever role you played, whatever work you did, made it possible for us to touch more than 27,000 patient lives in the nine plus years of its operation. And that doesn't include the positive impact for the patients' family members and the support provided to our staff. Please accept my heartfelt gratitude and know that you are one who chose to reach out in kindness to help those in need.

To the following people, I owe a debt of gratitude for the many roles you've played in my life, helping to bring the Healing Environments Program from dream, to concept, to reality.

Thank you so much for your love and support, for believing in me, even when I couldn't believe in myself.

My amazing husband Ron and our entire family

For their vision in seeing the possibilities of the Healing Environments Program at its concept level and furnishing everything required to nurture the program and enable it to provide comfort and compassion to the patients at St. Mary Medical Center for over nine years.

Lillian Schonewolf, Current: Trinity Mid-Atlantic Regional Vice President,
Community Health and Well-Being

Helen Gordon, Current: Fox Chase Cancer Center, Director of Volunteer Services
Former: St. Mary Medical Center, Assistant Director of Volunteer Services.

For helping me hold the dream and for continuing love and support, my heartfelt thanks to:

Donna Durbin

David Fernalld

Linda Morris-Brogan

Kathy Sterling

Diana Walker

MaryAnn Bryan

Jane Boyd Moughan

Gail R.

And for constant dedication:

Terry Beam

Carolyn Brown

Sonia Handa

Connie Hickey

Debbie and Kathryn

Sondra Holly

Lisa Bornachella

Lily Mollencott

Bill Cooper

And the volunteers at St. Mary Medical Center, especially those committed to

The Healing Environments Program

St. Mary Volunteer Department Staff

Joyce

Greg

The Sisters of St. Francis, St. Mary Medical Center

The Spiritual Care Department, St. Mary Medical Center

Yvette, Rickey, and Amy

The great staff at the Apple Store in Lawrenceville, NJ, who helped me make friends with my Mac so I could write this book!

Cantors Steven and Liz

Leslie, Rosita, the Brith Shalom Choir, and many loving, supportive friends at Congregation Brith Shalom, Houston, TX

Elayne Robinson Grossman

E.E.

Mark Malatesta, my wonderful author coach, The Bestselling Author, LLC. This book would never have become a reality without you, your knowledge and detailed guidance.

Nancy McCarthy, The Write Advantage, Project Manager extraordinaire

Frank Pronesti, Heirloom Studio, for your expertise behind the camera

Bowman Wildflower Preserve for creating "The Pond", photographed by Frank for my front cover

Stephanie Chandler, Laura West, and the marvelous staff at Authority Publishing

Sharla Brown and Jacquie Somerville, OneWoman, for your exceptional coaching skills, leadership, and encouragement.

To my manuscript readers, Steve Weinick and Carol Fenton. Thanks to you both for your marvelous suggestions.

To all who generously contributed their experiences and stories, the backbone of this book, I am deeply grateful.

The afghan draped over the bench on the front cover was created using Red Heart Super Saver Ombré yarn in color "Sunny".

Appendix I

The Sisters of St. Francis

Researched, Compiled, and Designed by Terri Rivera, Former Vice President, Community Health and Well-Being, St. Mary Medical Center and Marie Murphy Duess, author, speaker, graphic artist.

Photo courtesy of Nat Clymer

Appendix II

Healing Environments Questionnaire Responses

Shortly after starting the Healing Environments Program, we wanted to document feedback from the patients regarding how the program had made a difference in their St. Mary experience. We requested the addition of several questions to the Patient Satisfaction Reports sent to some patients after discharge. Unfortunately, we were informed that changing the form would be cost prohibitive. We did the next best thing and created our own questionnaire, which the Healing Ambassadors delivered to the patients. Included below are some of their comments.

Everything that was given to me is comfortable and practical. They will be useful, especially the squishy "under-the-arms bags." I will really use them at night to protect my breast stitches from harm. Thank you.

(*This patient had undergone a double mastectomy and was given two comfort "anti-ouch pillows" specially made by our American Sewing Guild members for breast cancer patients. The pillows can be worn anytime but are especially helpful at night and also in the car to provide protection and cushioning from seatbelts.)

The blanket I received kept me warm every single night (in the hospital). I used it over my shoulders as a robe for walking around the halls. I also received a heart pillow that soothed away my tummy pains.

When the Comfort Cart arrived, my mother's spirits were lifted as we kept vigil at my father's bedside. I would suggest you keep the program after its trial period. Cancer patients and their families need all the happiness they can get. We especially love the beautiful afghan. It's a visual reminder that lets my mom know someone cares.

I received a beautiful afghan and it brightens my bedroom and my day as I see it when I wake up. The volunteers were pleasant, and I enjoyed their visit. Thank you.

This is my first time here (at St. Mary). My nurses and staff were excellent. The gifts from the (Healing) Cart are beautiful. What a compassionate hospital!

The volunteers spoke with my husband and me like they'd known us a long time. The afghan colors work perfectly in our bedroom. The cart was filled with items both beautiful and practical for everyone.

Warm rays of sunshine, gift, prayers were all grate-fully received and appreciated. The ladies taking time to share and care with me (wife of the patient) was just what was needed—perfect timing. Thanks so much. God Bless. This program is wonderful—keep it going!

Right now, I am not at my best. The volunteers gave me not only gifts to make my stay more pleasant but also smiles, love, and such compassion. No words can describe my appreciation and gratitude. All I can say is THANK YOU and again thank you!

The volunteers who came to my room provided me with a radio so I could listen to my classical music and a panda bear for my granddaughter. I was given a beautiful colorful afghan. What a wonderful program you have at St. Mary. The people (the volunteers) pro-vide a wonderful service.

St. Mary has been wonderful; the staff, nurses, and volunteers are just fantastic. Friends visiting from out of town were so pleased with the great treatment that is given. Being in the hospital isn't a great visit but they've made it so comfortable.

Wow, what a blessing to have others care so much. This is truly being the hands and feet of Jesus! Please don't stop!

I was very impressed with the warmth and gener-osity shown with the gift cart visit. I have been sharing the experience with my family and friends.

I'll wear the beautiful scarf and shawl. I will tell people I know what a wonderful hospital this is. And this fantastic program provides warmth and love to the sick. I will come back to volunteer and participate in the (Healing Environments) program when I'm well.

Steve (husband) being given the blanket was such a lovely gesture. Thank you so much for putting a little joy into our day.

We received a blanket to keep my husband nice and warm and a puzzle book for me—both greatly appreciated. The visit from the healing volunteers absolutely made my day!

I have stage III cancer and have been receiving chemo for five years. I couldn't help but feel all the love and healing energy that went into making this most beautiful blanket of comfort. I am so grateful to the beautiful person (who made it) for her loving time and energies.

I found it very nice and comforting to receive the blanket and (neck roll) pillow. The service is a very good one for the patients here.

Thank you for being so kind to me. Your visit put a smile on my face at a time when I wasn't feeling well.

Your kindness and sincere concern gave my sister a feeling of warmth and love that seems to escape her at times. The volunteers made her feel important and the gifts gave her a very necessary lift that her sisters can't do. God bless you and keep you safe and healthy so you can continue bringing warmth and love to others.

I selected a multi-colored afghan from the cart. I opened the bag to remove it and started reading the blessing card. When I got to the last lines, "May the one who receives this afghan be cradled in hope, kept in joy, graced with peace, and wrapped in love," tears came to my eyes. This is a truly beautiful thing you're doing.

Volunteers Marilyn and Barbara were such a pleasure to see today. They made me feel special. I love the gifts the ladies had to offer, and they were very pleasurable to talk to. Every hospital should have great and friendly people like them!

My dad uses his healing blanket to keep warm at EVERY dialysis treatment, and he LOVES it!

What a surprise to have such a happy greeting and presents to warm my very hard transition to becoming a cancer patient.

The healing visit was a very pleasant experience and was very much appreciated. It was a generous and kind touch. Thank goodness for kind people.

I really needed a blanket! I was so cold, and it made me warmed physically and by the caring hands that made it and brought it.

I would personally like to thank the two volunteers who brightened my day by inviting me to choose a lovely afghan in sunny shades of yellow and a bedside pocket pouch for my phone and glasses. This blanket will forever hold a special place in my heart as I go through my journey. It will be "my blanket," the one I'll take to all my chemo infusions.

I've been in other hospitals, quite a few unfortunately, but St. Mary is something special!

Appendix III

Reources

1. **Prayer Shawl Ministry**
   www.shawlministry.com

2. **American Sewing Guild**
   National Headquarters
   9660 Hillcroft, Suite 510
   Houston, TX 77096
   713-729-3000 / 713-721-9230 Fax
   www.ASG.com
   360-220-8393

3. **Days for Girls International**
   PO Box 2622
   Mt. Vernon, WA 98273
   www.Daysforgirls.org

4. **Shoebox Ministry**
   13645 N. 32nd St
   Phoenix, AZ 85032
   480-905-1610
   Shoeboxministry.org

5. **On Eagle's Wings Ecumenical Ministries**
   10072 164th St
   Edmonton, AB T5P 4Y3
   Canada
   780-440-6594
   info@oneagleswings.org
   http://www.oneagleswings.org

6. **Handtied Fleece Blanket Instructions**
   (We made single layer blankets with1 ½ yards of fleece)
   www.Youtube.com How to make a tie blanket from fleece

7. **Warm Up America Foundation**
   m.facebook.com/WarmUpAmerica